MARKHAM

"Markham's Enterprises"
by Mike Krunic and Wendy Priesnitz

Produced in co-operation with
The Markham Board of Trade

Windsor Publications, Ltd.
Burlington, Ontario

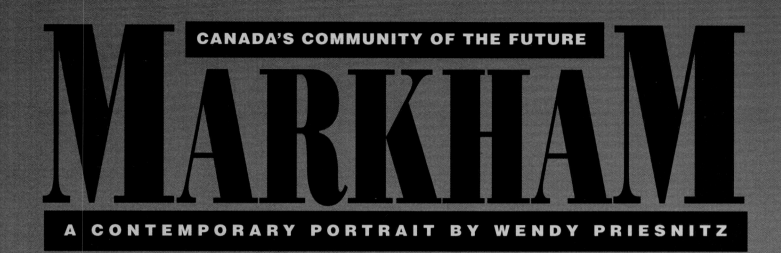

CANADA'S COMMUNITY OF THE FUTURE
MARKHAM
A CONTEMPORARY PORTRAIT BY WENDY PRIESNITZ

Windsor Publications, Ltd.—Book Division

Managing Editor: Karen Story

Design Director: Alexander E. D'Anca

Photo Director: Susan L. Wells

Executive Editor: Pamela Schroeder

Staff for *Markham: Canada's Community of the Future*

Manuscript Editor: Doreen Nakakihara

Photo Editor: Cameron Cox

Senior Editor, Corporate Profiles: Judith L. Hunter

Production Editor, Corporate Profiles: Una FitzSimons

Co-ordinator, Corporate Profiles: Gladys McKnight

Editorial Assistants: Phyllis Feldman-Schroeder, Kim Kievman, Michael Nugwynne, Michele Oakley, Kathy B. Peyser, Susan Schlanger, Theresa J. Solis

Publisher's Representatives, Corporate Profiles: David Mills, Angela Schillum

Layout Artist, Corporate Profiles: Bonnie Felt

Designer: Ellen Ifrah

Windsor Publications, Ltd.

Elliot Martin, Chairman of the Board

James L. Fish III, Chief Operating Officer

Michele Sylvestro, Vice President/Sales-Marketing

Mac Buhler, Vice President/Sponsor Acquisitions

ISBN: 0-89781-327-8

Contents

PART I
Canada's Community of the Future
13

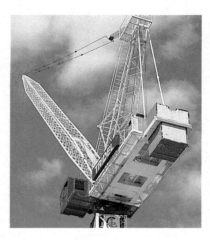

PART II
Markham's Enterprises
119

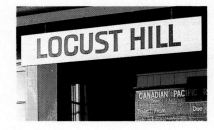

Acknowledgments

I am grateful to all of those individuals and organizations who supplied me with informal interviews, research assistance, technical information, and suggestions.

Special thanks to Mayor Tony Roman and his staff, Ethel Luhtanen at the Markham Board of Trade, and staff of the Markham Public Library and the Markham Museum. Appreciation also goes to the many dynamic Markham companies profiled here, for their time and gracious co-operation.

Most of all, I appreciate the patience and support of Pam Schroeder, Doreen Nakakihara, and Gladys McKnight at Windsor Publications.

LEFT: Autumn drapes the Markham landscape in hues of red and gold. Photo by Pete Ryan. Courtesy, First Light

Pictured here is the 1989-1990 Board of Directors of the Markham Board of Trade.

Courtesy, Markham Board of Trade/Lorne Chapman Photography Inc.

President's Message

When we look around our community today, we can scarcely imagine what it was like 100 years ago. Nor can we fully appreciate how much it has changed over the years. As you look through the pages of this book, however, perhaps our past and our progress will be easier to trace.

Even the settlers who founded Markham—undoubtedly with a healthy share of vision and foresight—probably had little idea that our community would emerge as one of the largest industrial growth areas in Canada. That growth, even over the past two decades, has been remarkable.

Markham was built not only on the pioneering vision of yesterday, but on the entrepreneurial spirit of today. Both those characteristics are clearly evident in the Markham Board of Trade—we owe just as much to the dedication and hard work of our volunteers as our community does to those first settlers who began building it.

Our growth at the Board mirrors the growth of Markham itself. Since our formation in 1981, our membership has grown from its original 30 to well over 1,200 members. All of the organization, planning, and creativity necessary to meet members' ongoing needs is supplied by a supportive office staff operating out of our beautiful new headquarters, which all of us are extremely proud of.

This progress has been made possible by our volunteers, who, together, have succeeded in building the Board from the ground up.

Stephen Leacock, one of Canada's best-loved humorists, would have appreciated their industry and co-operation. Their success gives new meaning to his familiar observation: "I am a great believer in luck. And I find the harder I work, the more I have of it."

This book celebrates Markham. It belongs to our entire community. As you read it, you will realize that the vision of the past is translated in the achivements of the present, and in our hopes for the future.

On behalf of the Markham Board of Trade, I am proud to present it to you.

Karen Mugford, President
Markham Board of Trade

MARKHAM
COMMUNITY
LIBRARY

PART

I

Canada's Community
of the Future

William Markham, after whom Markham is named, was the Archbishop of York, England, from 1777 to 1807. Courtesy, Markham District Historical Museum

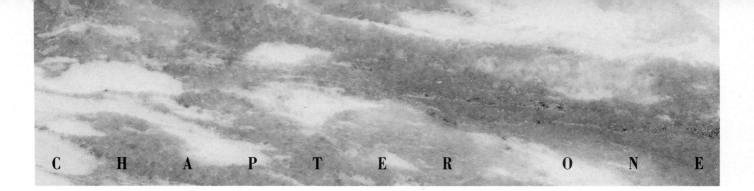

At the Crossroads

The late winter afternoon sun glints blindingly off the curved glass sides of the Allstate corporate headquarters. At the crossroads of the Town of Markham's two main thoroughfares, row upon row of reflected rush hour headlights mirror a bustling economy and an impatience for growth.

Not more than a few miles away, the same sun appears older and slower. It casts long shadows and bathes the row of charming, clapboard buildings with window-boxed geraniums in a warm, golden glow. Everything about this village scene conspires to transport the visitor back in time a few hundred years in a search for the town's roots.

But this gentle, pastoral picture belies Markham's true origins, which have more in common with the frenzied development and grit of modern highways and granite towers.

Ever since 1793, when the Township of Markham was first surveyed, the area's history has been forged by individuals with a strong vision and a pioneering attitude. From the early settlers to those who have more recently contributed to the town's status as one of the most affluent and fast-growing municipalities in Canada, there has been a strength of purpose and a degree of bravery sufficient to take the right fork at each crossroads in the town's development.

The Immigration

Modern Markham is a haven for land developers. But none of today's developers, no matter how skilled or aggressive, are as audacious as was the area's first developer, a dashing German aristocrat named William Berczy.

A scholar, architect, and painter as well as an adventurer and explorer, this enterprising man had, around 1790, recruited 200 Germans to settle in upper New York State as part of a British settlement program. When conditions in New York proved unsatisfactory, Berczy became interested in an aggressive settlement policy sponsored by Upper Canada's lieutenant-governor, Colonel John Graves Simcoe.

Simcoe's policy was designed to attract high-quality settlers from Europe who were eager to escape from the hardships of war and political upheaval that pervaded Europe in the eighteenth century. It offered grants of 200 acres to anyone willing and able to clear five of the acres, build a house, and create a road in front.

Simcoe particularly had his eye on the Dutch and German immigrants who were already settled in New York and Pennsylvania. These people were recognized as self-sufficient and highly successful settlers. (And, indeed, many of them did travel to Markham in their conestoga wagons. Their descendants still farm the ever-decreasing but rich farmland north of the town.)

Berczy had originally asked Simcoe for a grant of a million acres to accommodate a grandiose settlement that would be populated by thousands of future immigrants, but after a good deal of negotiating, he accepted 64,000 acres. So it was that 200 people spent the winter of 1794-95 in primitive log houses in the forests of Markham Township.

The following few years were hard ones for the relocated Berczy settlers, who were plagued by crop failure and disease. The developer's vision faltered in the face of a variety of political roadblocks, and his finances fell into ruin. By the turn of the nineteenth century, Berczy was broken-hearted and bankrupt, having lost a title battle for the lands he had settled.

Meanwhile, other nationalities were also finding new homes in the wilds of Markham Township. A small number of French clerics and aristocrats had fled the French Revolution to England, and they arrived in Upper Canada after the British government orchestrated a mass immigration. But many of them later returned to France, decidedly lacking in the ability to rough it.

A number of English, Irish, and Scottish settlers also immigrated to Markham, having fled the hardships of industrialization and famine in their homelands.

The Development
Just as strong transportation networks support the strength of modern Markham, rivers and roads were a crucial factor in the early development of the township.

This photo shows a group of unidentified farmers clearing land in early Markham for future cultivation. Courtesy, Markham District Historical Museum

A large portion of Markham Township is drained by the Rouge River and its network of streams, which eventually trickle down to enter Lake Ontario in neighboring Pickering Township. The river has had a number of names including *Katabokakonk,* which meant "river of easy entrance" to the Iroquois Indians who used its valley as a portage to the north prior to the coming of the settlers. The name "Rouge" likely came from the deposits of red clay which sometimes color the water.

Now seen as little more than a scenic stream winding through built-up subdivisions of Markham and Unionville, the Rouge River played an important part in the development of the area. Because the waterway is fast flowing, a variety of mills

sprang up on its banks. Twelve water mills were reported to exist on the Rouge in 1817. The river also may have been used for transportation, because Berczy settlers Philip Eckardt and his wife are said to have travelled by boat up the Rouge to their grant south of Unionville.

Near what is now the village of Unionville, the enterprising Berczy cleared the banks of the river and built a warehouse, hoping to add to the prosperity of his planned settlement by attracting the attention of fur traders. Although the fur traders didn't respond to Berczy's scheme, by the mid-nineteenth century a bustling little hamlet developed along the Sixth Line, which later would become Unionville's Main Street. There was a grist mill, a sawmill, and two inns, as well as a weaver, a shoemaker, a tailor, two carpenters, and a blacksmith.

Other members of Berczy's hardy group arrived in

LEFT: Local waters, such as the Rouge River, were a natural form of energy for a variety of mills that sprang up in the Markham area. Pictured here is Milne's Dam and the Milne grist mill. Courtesy, Markham District Historical Museum

OPPOSITE, TOP: Some of the earliest enterprises in the township of Markham were sawmills and planing mills. This lumber wagon was pictured on Station Lane, Unionville, in 1904. Courtesy, Markham District Historical Museum

OPPOSITE, BOTTOM: These members of a threshing crew posed for this picture on Reesor's farm in Locust Hill in 1902. Courtesy, Markham District Historical Museum

Markham Township from York by travelling up a smaller river, the Don. On its banks they established a tiny settlement named German Mills, near the present-day intersection of John Street and Don Mills Road. A grist mill and a number of other small enterprises prospered for a few years, until it became clear that the river's power was insufficient and the settlement declined.

As Markham Township developed, so did the need for supplementary travel routes. Unfortunately, the very river that had helped to open up the interior of the township also hindered the development of road networks. Because the Rouge was so fast flowing, it was difficult to bridge. Roads were often built in meandering curves to follow the river, or were made to jog off the straight course in order to reach a narrow crossing place. During the spring run-off the river often overflowed its banks, turning roadways into muddy swamps. As late as 1880, travellers

The community of Markham has long been conscious of the quality of their roads. Here a crew resurfaces Main Street, in Unionville, in 1904. Courtesy, Markham District Historical Museum

described the roads of Markham Township as "terrible."

Probably the road most important to the development of Markham, and one of the first to be improved, was Yonge Street. As early as 1794, Lieutenant-Governor Simcoe had realized the importance of the road that still forms the town's western border. Recognizing a need for a direct military route to Lake Simcoe and points north, he spearheaded a project which employed settlers to help build a road out of what was little better than a primitive Indian trail slashed through the bush. Berczy supplied men to assist in the project.

Further improvements were made to the Yonge Street trail in the early 1800s by the North West Company, which began to

use it as a transportation artery for the fur trade. Then during the War of 1812, the roadway was used to transport military equipment and supplies.

Once Yonge Street was cleared, lots were sold along its length, creating a village that was eventually named Thornhill after local merchant Benjamin Thorne. As the condition of the road improved, businesses began to open and flourish. One early enterprise, located at the intersection of Yonge Street and what is now Highway 7, was owned by John Langstaff. In 1840 he ran a store, pail factory, and eavestrough and shingle mill on the site.

The Village of Thornhill became the largest milling centre

Laura and Clara Reesor posed for this winter image taken along Main Street, in Markham, in 1906. Visible in the distance are the Franklin House and, to its left, the Town Hall. Courtesy, Markham District Historical Museum

north of York, a position that was short-lived. By the middle of the century, political conditions and the increasing importance of York caused business in Thornhill to slow considerably. In spite of this hardship, the village continued to grow, and by the late 1840s had a post office, stagecoach service, a toll gate, four churches, and two schools.

While Yonge Street was being developed, Simcoe also had the settlers cut a number of roads into the interior of the township. One of the earliest trails ran off Yonge Street, approximately along the route of present-day John Street, to the settlement of German Mills. It was known for a time as the Mill Road. Then in the 1850s it was planked and called the Pomona Plank Road. In 1864 the township council surfaced the road with stone, creating the first so-called "macadam" road in the township.

Another sideroad was cleared along the route of the present Highway 7 as far as the Eighth Line, which is now known as Highway 48 or Main Street in the village of Markham. This facilitated the development of the core of the Berczy settlement at Unionville, although parts of this road south of the village were so low and swampy that travellers usually detoured north to the next sideroad (now 16th Avenue). The problem was eventually remedied by laying tree trunks side by side to create "corduroy roads," but as a result, the village of Unionville developed some distance north of the main crossroads.

Corduroy roads were bone-shaking, to say the least. And because macadamizing was expensive, planking became the accepted method of making main roads passable year-round. The Markham and Scarborough Plank Company was formed in 1852, supplied by sawmills along the route. In order to offset the cost of replacing broken planks every 10 years or so, toll gates were set up at various spots along the planked roads.

Just as roadways replaced rivers as the impetus to Markham's growth, for one glorious era at the turn of the century, railways took their place at the centre of the development stage. A variety of companies laid tracks across the township.

When the Toronto and Nipissing Railway was formed in 1868, the township promptly encouraged the company to undertake the massive task of routing a line in its direction. The railroad brought a temporary boom to the village of Markham and later became part of the Canadian National system.

The Ontario Simcoe and Huron Railway came to the Yonge Street corridor in 1853, and the Ontario and Quebec Railway (known later as the Canadian Pacific Railway) arrived in the eastern section of the township in the 1880s.

The Maturation
Yet another era in Markham's development history was ushered in by the construction of an electric radial railway system along

The railroad ushered in a new age of growth for the village of Markham. Pictured is the Grand Trunk Railroad Station. Courtesy, Markham District Historical Museum

Yonge Street. Allowing people from Toronto to move north of the city's boundaries and travel into the city each day to work, this new form of rapid transit created the area's first commuters. By 1899 the Metropolitan Radial Railway was making five trips a day in both directions up and down Yonge Street, a run that was to last until the 1930s when the line was replaced by buses.

The commuter phenomenon was, of course, one that steadily increased with the advent of the automobile. As the first half of the twentieth century ticked away, the local newspaper showed Markham to be a rural village already experiencing some of the problems of urban growth.

On November 30, 1939, a *Markham Economist and Sun* reporter wrote:

With no blame attached to the Constable who finds it impossible to always be Johnny on the Spot, rules and regulations of the village are continuously being ignored. With dogs running at large, bicycles traversing the sidewalks and cars speeding along Main Street at fifty or sixty miles per hour, people never know when they are safe. On Sunday while church attendants were leaving the churches, a car sped north at a tremendous speed regardless of the extra amount of traffic at that hour or the danger incurred.

The rest of the paper contained news about the Women's Institutes, a report on a Junior Farmers girls' project entitled "The Art of Being Well Dressed and Well Groomed," farm news, and tips on how to fatten turkeys.

In 1939 building permits for 21 new dwellings were issued by the township, and newspaper accounts noted that many wealthy people were locating there because of low taxes, good roads, and building by-laws.

By the end of World War II, Markham's population significantly began to expand through what was to become a continuous flow of people from Toronto. The villages of Markham, Unionville, and Thornhill turned into bedroom communities filled with families trying to escape Metropolitan Toronto's urbanization.

By 1950 the *Economist and Sun*'s editorial writer was bemoaning the fact that Markham Village was facing heavy expenditures and rising taxes due to an increasing population that required "more schools, increased fire protection, new council chambers, substantial extension of water service, new roads and sidewalks."

When township reeve Stewart Rumble addressed the first council meeting of 1967, he predicted a "fine outlook and rapid change" for Markham as it entered Canada's second century. But it is unlikely that even he imagined that the area's property tax assessment would almost double between 1971 and 1979. By 1977 newspaper headlines were proclaiming, "Planners Anticipate Boom Development."

It is unlikely that anyone, least of all pioneer developer William Berczy, could have imagined that Markham would become the highly affluent, sophisticated urban centre that it is today. But by the 1980s an enterprising group of pioneers, developers, residents, politicians, and businesspeople had made Markham a prosperous world-class municipality—its abundant office towers, retail malls, and industrial parks balancing its exclusive and expensive residential areas.

And the future seems to hold no reduction in the growth and prosperity. As Alex Barton, Markham's treasurer and industrial commissioner for nearly 27 years until his retirement in 1988, was fond of saying, "The sun always shines on Markham."

The Markham Fire Brigade posed for this image in front of the Town Hall on May 1, 1895. Courtesy, Markham District Historical Museum

In the latter half of the 1980s development applications in Markham reached an all-time
high, and nearly 5,000 building permits were issued for more than $650 million worth of
construction. Photo by Glen Jones

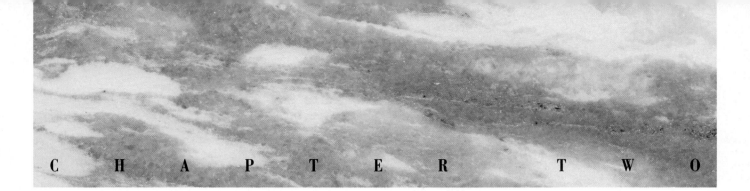

A Commitment to Growth

From Lieutenant-Governor Simcoe's settlement policy which first attracted pioneers to the Markham area in the 1700s to the town's current aggressive economic development department, government policies have always encouraged people and commerce to move to Markham.

The town's governing structure has undergone many changes in the past two centuries in order to adjust to and foster the development that has shaped modern Markham. Indeed, there was no local government to help the Berczy settlers establish their Rouge River Valley homesteads.

Magistrates of the Home District, appointed by the lieutenant-governor in York (later to be renamed Toronto) and by annual town meetings, were in charge. They controlled funds and provided the first government services, mostly geared toward keeping the peace. The primitive roads that the settlers had cleared in order to gain title to their plots of land were also maintained under the jurisdiction of the magistrates, and new ones gradually developed. Otherwise, the pioneers relied on their own sweat, and that of their neighbours, to survive.

At first even voting took a great deal of effort, as voters had to make the difficult journey to York. Votes were not secret and elections often featured violence, voter intimidation, and even riots. Gradually, party affiliations began to develop as people organized themselves into the Tory and Reform parties and power became focused in a Legislative Assembly.

The struggle between the two differing points of view came to a head in 1837. A firebrand politician and champion of the oppressed named William Lyon MacKenzie led local farmers in an unsuccessful revolt against the Family Compact, a small group that monopolized the central government.

Many Markham Township men played a part in the drama, on both sides of the battleground, and are immortalized in the names of local streets: Major John Button, Major George Denison, Colonel Moody, and Benjamin Milliken on the side of law and order, and families like the Eckardts, Hemmingways, Stivers, Ramers, Reesors, and Milnes on the Reform side. The reform tradition survived for many years at the upper levels of government, although modern Markham has become politically more conservative.

By the 1840s the system of home districts and magistrates had become an unwieldy method of local governance. So it was replaced with a system of county and township councils, by which the County of York and the Township of Markham were formed.

The Villages Develop

The various settlements within the township developed at their own speeds and in different ways. Thornhill (so named when its post office opened in 1829) had a population of about 700, mostly living along Yonge Street, by the mid-nineteenth century. Although it had its share of economic ups and downs, Thornhill's location on the main thoroughfare ensured its steady growth.

In contrast, the early development of the hamlet of Unionville occured away from the roadway, only to be extended south in later years when the railway and Highway 7 were constructed. (As a consequence of this pattern of growth, much of the nineteenth-century village still remains intact today.) Unionville wasn't formalized as a police village until 1907.

Markham Village was incorporated in 1872, after a series of catastrophic fires convinced its 750 residents of the need to finance the purchase of fire equipment through tax collection. At the same time, the village's development was aided greatly by the coming of the railroad. The first train passed through in 1871 and the Toronto and Nipissing Railway built stations in both Markham and Unionville at a cost of $1,800 and $1,450 respectively.

During the first half of the twentieth century, the village, township, and county structures continued to serve the needs of the slowly but steadily growing rural population. However by 1950, due to a continuous postwar flow of people relocating from Toronto, the township's population and subsequent demand for services began to increase more quickly, necessitating construction of a new municipal building in Buttonville.

Then in 1971 another reorganization of the municipal government structure occurred in order to accommodate growth. The York County Council, having observed the success of the two-tier regional government system of its huge urban neighbour to the south, Metropolitan Toronto, petitioned the provincial government to do the same in York County. So on January 1, 1971, the Regional Municipality of York was incorporated with the Town of Markham as one of its eight local components.

The Regional Council, made up of representatives from lower-level town councils, provides health and community services, police protection, and water and sewage services, and is responsible for regional roads.

Other municipal services such as planning and by-laws, public transit, parks and recreation, fire protection, tax collection, industrial development, and garbage collection are taken care of by the Town of Markham. The Markham Council comprises the mayor, four regional councillors (who, along with the mayor, represent Markham's interests on the Regional Council of York), and councillors representing each of the town's eight wards.

With incorporation, a vision emerged of Markham as a self-sufficient town. Tempered by the desire of town staff, elected officials, and residents to keep its identity separate from that of Metro Toronto, Markham was set on a course that would take it far beyond its roots as a sleepy rural town and its days as a bedroom community for the big city.

While under construction, Markham's city hall resembled an abstract sculpture. Photo by Glen Jones

Large tracts of land began to become available for development and, with a relatively low tax base and a progressive council, things began to happen. Work soon began on an Official Plan, approved in 1976, that set the pattern for the future growth that was considered inevitable.

Policies were needed to help residents move around their growing town. A lot had happened in Markham since the installation, in 1950, of the first stoplight at the busy intersection of Main Street and Highway 7. In the 1970s the first Markham Transit buses began to wind through the streets, down Markham Road, along Highway 7 to Unionville, and down Kennedy Road to connect with a Toronto bus at Steeles Avenue. Over the years service has continually expanded to meet residents' needs: first bus shelters, then evening and Saturday service, increased routes, more buses, Sunday service, and improved connections with the transit services of the surrounding municipalities.

Markham Hydro is another municipal service that has worked hard to keep pace with the town's rapid growth. Only in business since 1979, it is now Ontario's 16th-largest utility and has an annual growth rate of 15 percent. Its modern head office is both futuristic in design and efficient in operation, indicative of its innovating style.

The service that has had the most influence on Markham's growth is sewage treatment. A 16,000-person-capacity system completed in 1960 soon reached its limit. To allow for further growth, in the late 1970s the town connected up with the York-

Durham Servicing Scheme (referred to affectionately as "The Big Pipe"), a massive sewage collection and treatment system that culminates in a treatment plant at Lake Ontario in adjacent Durham Region.

Open for Business

Markham's leaders in the 1960s were aware that the future was bright for the town. A newspaper report described a meeting with a local developer to discuss a program of industrial development for the village. The company had prepared a large map with a circle colored in yellow, dubbed "the Golden Circle." It had a radius of 10 miles from the hub of Markham Village and the report stated, "The area encompassed in the circle indicates that this village is strategically located for industrial growth."

By 1970 the Markham Council had a stated intention to continue to attract industry. It embarked on a program of staged installation of roads and services well in advance of actual demand, a planning policy which greatly added to Markham's competitiveness in attracting industry.

The council's approach to growth continues to be businesslike and progressive. In setting annual budgets, whether $2,500 in 1864 or $55 million in 1988, the need for debt has been eliminated by a pay-as-you-go philosophy which sustains new development. Lot levies pay for residential necessities such as fire halls, libraries, and recreation facilities. In fact, this fiscal policy has actually reduced the per capita debt during these years of growth, from $190 in 1970 to $47 in 1987.

As more evidence of fiscal responsibility, Markham has a long history of low taxes. In fact, in 1939 and 1940, taxes were slightly lowered while the township council tried to find places to spend its surplus cash. While today's fast rate of growth ensures that there will be no surplus at the end of the year, careful planning continues to mean no or small increases for property taxpayers. And low industrial realty taxes (the lowest of 10 metro municipalities during the past few years) have added to the list of things that make Markham attractive to the business sector.

There is no wizardry in holding the line on taxes; it is accomplished by the town's businesslike approach to growth. The growth of the industrial and commercial sectors has been successfully controlled by Official Plan monitoring policies adopted to balance the desired assessment ratio between industrial/commercial and residential to ensure the continuance of the existing economical tax rates. In 1970 the council announced its intention to aim for a 40:60 industrial to residential ratio. The assessment growth pattern has steadily increased from 19:81 in 1971 to 29:71 in 1987.

Much of the credit for both the growth and the businesslike tone is generally given to Tony Roman, who was mayor during the early growth years of the 1970s. Roman's successor, Carole Bell, who worked with him as a councillor from 1972 until she took over as mayor when he was elected chairman of York Region in 1984, continued the pro-development style.

The policy of balancing commercial and residential assessment was set in place by successive councils and executed by a man who held the dual roles of treasurer and industrial commissioner for close to three decades. Alex Barton was well known for his unabashed promotion of the town.

Through Barton and his successor, the town has actively persuaded many companies to move to Markham. There is an

annual advertising campaign, and the town is represented at events where Canadian and foreign companies gather to investigate business opportunities. The industrial commissioner also periodically investigates Canada's regions and the offshore business scene, running a soft-sell campaign.

Along with his colleagues in other departments and the Markham Council, Barton developed a tradition of working closely with business and industry, looking into companies' needs, and helping them through all stages from site selection to the final completion of buildings.

These strategies have been very successful. A diversity of commerce has resulted, with an emphasis on clean manufacturing, high tech, and corporate head offices. From 1971 to 1984 the town's industrial and commercial value increased tenfold to $2 billion, while its residential value tripled to $3 billion.

And there is no end in sight. In his *Year End Report for 1987*, Planning Director Tom Januszewski noted that development applications had reached an all-time high that year, representing a 42.5 percent increase over the previous year. Almost 5,000

building permits were issued for more than $650 million worth of construction, with commercial and industrial permits accounting for one-fifth of the value.

Support for Business

Organizations like the Markham Board of Trade have worked hand-in-hand with the municipal government to promote business development in Markham. The Board of Trade is a relatively new entity, having been launched in 1981 with less than 100 members, but it has grown quickly to a membership of more than 1,000 companies. Following in the footsteps of the old chamber of commerce, which began on Markham's Main Street in 1952, it is representative of the diverse business composition of the town. Members come from all sectors and include small businesses as well as the area's large corporations.

As part of the extended network made up of the Ontario and Canadian chambers of commerce, the Board of Trade is able to ensure that the interests of the Markham business community are represented in policy discussions at all levels of gov-

OPPOSITE: Markham Hydro's modern head office is futuristic in design and efficient in operation. Photo by Dawn Goss. Courtesy, First Light

BELOW: Three framed structures await completion in a Markham neighbourhood. Photo by Glen Jones

Lovely residential neighbourhoods fill the Markham area. Courtesy, Mel Reid & Associates

ernment. In addition to being an effective vehicle for communicating with the municipal government about local business issues, the Board of Trade has developed a broader focus which includes such tasks as helping members to strategize about international trade.

The Board also hosts a small business information centre in its offices and provides members with regular opportunities for exchanging information about the products and services available in Markham. Services to members also include a business awards program; a variety of publications such as a monthly newsletter, an annual directory, and a tourism guide; and educational programs geared to small business.

Perhaps the most significant aspect of industrial and com-

mercial growth in Markham has been its emergence as a major focus for high-tech firms. This has been encouraged in recent years by the York Technology Association (YTA). Founded in 1983 by MPP Don Cousens, formerly an executive with Honeywell Ltd., and Peter Baines, president of locally based Mohawk Data Sciences Canada Limited, the association received a $100,000 start-up grant from the Town of Markham. The money was allocated for the development of incentive programs to attract additional high-tech companies to town.

Markham has recently emerged as a major focus for high-tech firms such as IBM. Photo by Jack Holman

The YTA quickly became self-sustaining and is now the largest high-tech organization in Canada, with a membership list that is an impressive "who's who" of the industry. The group interacts with all levels of government and with other national trade associations, supporting initiatives that are beneficial to

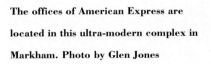

The offices of American Express are located in this ultra-modern complex in Markham. Photo by Glen Jones

the industry.

Also influential in spreading the word about Markham as a desirable location for business is the Metro North Business Show. Produced by local councillor and businessman Fred Cox, it is a trade show, created to provide the business sector with its own forum for major marketing opportunities. Held annually in October since 1988, it has quickly developed into a high-calibre event which has attracted all facets of business from the Markham and greater Toronto areas. Representatives of both large and small companies, as well as interested members of the general public, attend to learn of business in Markham.

As all this activity paves the way for future growth and development, the town's planners are constantly having to anticipate future trends and adjust to current ones. For example, as a result of a study conducted in 1983 which identified a general shift from industrial-type jobs toward office-type activities, the planning department recommended zoning changes designed to create more office space. This formed the basis for the development of a commercial core of office towers and support services dedicated to business, and attracted a number of corporate head offices.

In order to serve its burgeoning corporate and residential populations, the municipal government also has had to grow. To accommodate this, construction began in 1988 on an exciting new civic centre to replace the 1950s-vintage facility which

had long been bursting at the seams. Located on 26 acres at the corner of Warden Avenue and Highway 7 and worth an estimated $22.5 million, the 150,000-square-foot complex was designed by distinguished Canadian architect Arthur Erickson. The design features reflecting ponds, pillars, extensive glazing, hanging gardens, and a winter garden. Facilities include new council chambers with seating for 200 residents, a cafeteria, a day-care centre, a large atrium for receptions, and a chapel.

The civic centre will, through many more years of growth, provide an efficient workplace for the town's thousands of employees while acting as a high-profile focal point worthy of the world-class municipality that Markham has become. It also will provide a gathering place for local residents, epitomizing the feeling of community that is so important to the people of Markham.

ABOVE AND OPPOSITE: Small shops and boutiques add to the Markham area's commercial diversity and draw shoppers to Main Street. Courtesy, Mel Reid & Associates; Glen Jones

Sheathed in reflective silver and blue glass with aluminum panels, Scotia Bank's Commercial Tower contains 168,500 square feet of office space. Photo by Jack Holman

An Enterprising Town

From mill wheel to soaring skyscraper, Markham has developed into a prosperous community with pioneer roots and challenging prospects. The exciting spirit of modern Markham has attracted more than 4,000 businesses which, true to a long tradition of industry and commerce, are helping it along the road to self-sufficiency.

As the area's earliest settlers began to build their homes and produce their food, they set up rudimentary mills for grinding flour and creating planks from logs. They were fortunate to have at their disposal many fast-flowing streams, and both sawmills and grist mills appeared early in the 1800s. Virtually every little developing hamlet had at least one mill at its core. Sawmills were especially abundant as the building of railways, the planking of roads, and the building of houses created a booming market for lumber.

This replica of the Unionville Planing Mill houses restaurants and boutiques. The original mill, after surviving for more than 100 years, was destroyed by fire in 1978. Photo by Glen Jones

The Heritage

The village of Thornhill owes both its name and early prosperity to a miller named Benjamin Thorne. Thorne was an energetic entrepreneur who exported his flour to Britain, creating a healthy market for wheat being grown in the area. A second mill complex on John Street named Pomona Mills, which could produce 45,000 barrels of flour a year, helped attract more business to the prospering village.

Mills were also important to villages in the eastern part of the township. The Milne Mills, also known as Markham Mills, located just south of Highway 7 on McCowan Road, included a woollen mill, an ashery, a sawmill, and a grist mill as well as a general store. One generation of the Milne family, believing that a new dam could be used to generate power for the village, built a steel and concrete dam, the first of its kind in the area.

The village of Unionville also owes its existence to mills. In the 1840s a flour mill, called Union Mills, was built at the south end of the bridge over the Rouge River. The lane into the mill would eventually become Main Street, but the mill met a fate common to many and was destroyed by fire in 1934. Also in Unionville was a planing mill, a successful business well into the twentieth century supplying lumber, doors, and frames for local buildings. After surviving in its

original condition for more than 100 years, the mill was destroyed by fire in 1978. A decade later a replica, aptly named the Unionville Planing Mill, was built in its place to house a restaurant and boutiques.

Along with the mills, a variety of other enterprises sprang up. One such business was barrel making. Often a cooper's shop would be attached to a mill, and the census of 1851 lists at least 16 of these tradesmen in the township. Another very important artisan in the early days of Markham Township was

Markham's Highway 7 facilitates east-west travel in the area. Photo by Winston Fraser

the blacksmith, not only for shoeing horses and oxen but also for making small farm and household implements. Many of the blacksmiths developed their businesses into larger manufacturing enterprises, producing wagons, cutters, and buggies.

In this way, the main street of the village of Markham had become home to a number of factories by the middle of the nineteenth century. One such enterprise, the Speight Carriage Works, on Main Street just north of Highway 7, employed 125 men. The business gradually declined at the turn of the century, but the building remained standing until 1976. Other partners in the industrial development of Markham were James Robinson, who in 1886 set up the Maple Leaf Woollen Mills in a tall brick building in the village, and Stephen Peer, who founded a foundry that produced bells.

With all of this manufacturing activity, Markham became known as "the Birmingham of Ontario" after the industrial boom town in England. Since the employees of these industries required homes and services, a strong commercial and service sector also developed.

This prosperity was bolstered for a few years by the coming of the railway. Farmers sent logs, grain, cattle, hogs, and milk off to market and local industries shipped their products to cus-

LEFT: A Canadian National Railway train passes through Markham. Canada's transcontinental railway system's major east-west lines and main marshalling yards are located only minutes from Markham. Photo by Glen Jones

BELOW: Toronto-Buttonville International Airport, situated just north of the Highway 7 and Highway 404 interchange, is ideally located to serve both Markham and Toronto. Photo by Winston Fraser

tomers in other areas. But gradually many of the Markham industries fell victim to larger competitors, and commerce declined.

The Boom

In the first half of the twentieth century, Markham continued to have a rural economy. Then in the late 1970s, an unprecedented influx of business from across the country and abroad transformed Markham from a rural municipality to a significant business centre.

The businesses, both large and small, that have relocated, expanded, or begun operations in Markham chose the town for a variety of reasons besides favorable municipal government policies. These include its accessible location and availability of serviced industrial land at competitive prices.

One of the major propellants of this growth is an excellent transportation network. By road, rail, or air, Markham is among the most accessible municipalities in southern Ontario. It is within a day's trucking of 120 million customers and 56 percent of North America's industrial market. Located on the northern boundary of Canada's largest metropolitan concentration of people, Markham's major road network connects directly with Metro Toronto's. Highway 404 provides direct access to Highway 401 and the Don Valley Parkway. Markham's major north-south streets also provide access to Toronto, while Steeles Avenue, 16th Avenue, and Highway 7 facilitate east-west travel.

Road reconstruction projects are continuously upgrading these and other important internal roadways. When construction is completed on Highway 407, a major east-west route through the southern York Region, Markham's road system will be further able to accommodate the increased traffic generated by development.

Greatly enhancing this transportation network is the Toronto-Buttonville International Airport. Begun as a meagre grass strip in 1940, it has been developed into a first-class facility totally without public funds. Located just north of the Highway 7/404 interchange, Buttonville is ideally located to serve both Markham and Toronto. It is one of the most complete general aviation facilities in Canada and acts as a satellite airport for

Parkway Corporate Centre, an imposing glass-and-steel highrise, stands in Markham. Photo by Winston Fraser

Lester B. Pearson International Airport, located near Toronto's western boundary but only five minutes away from Markham by corporate jet. Since its tower opened in 1967, it has consistently ranked among the top 12 busiest airports in the country, with an average of more than 200,000 takeoffs and landings each year. Today more than 300 aircraft call it home, and the number continues to grow as new industries locate in Markham.

In addition to good road and air access, Markham enjoys excellent railway service. The major east-west lines as well as the main marshalling yards of Canada's transcontinental railway system are only minutes from Markham. In addition, commuters are well served by provincial "GO" Transit routes.

One of the earliest companies to realize that Markham is the place to be was Steelcase Canada, a designer and manufacturer of office furnishings. In 1955 it relocated from Don Mills to a street, near Steeles and Woodbine avenues, that the town

OPPOSITE, TOP: The head office of Allstate Insurance consists of a 10-storey, black-glass building and a central silo that soars above two stepped wings. Photo by Jack Holman

OPPOSITE, BOTTOM: Valleywood Business Park is located within walking distance of the Apple Creek Centre. Photo by Jack Holman

LEFT: Honeywell has helped contribute to Markham's reputation as "Canada's Silicon Valley." This building is located on Birchmount Road. Photo by Jack Holman

named after it. Two other corporate pioneers relocated to Markham in 1957: Emerson Electric Canada Limited and Chesebrough-Pond's (Canada) Inc. The latter company, a cosmetic manufacturer, moved into a 56,000-square-foot manufacturing and office facility at the end of a dirt road that would become Bullock Drive. Surrounded at first by farms and fields, the firm grew with the community to become a successful multifaceted corporation and a strong Markham supporter.

One of the town's first industrial subdivisions was Markham Industrial Park, located in the Heritage Road/McCowan Road area north of Highway 7. It was developed by Western Heritage Ltd. in the late 1960s. C.I.P. Containers Ltd. opened a 126,000-square-foot plant there in 1968. The $3.8-million, fully integrated corrugated container plant is situated on 15 acres and employed 200 people when it opened.

With the escalating pace of development in Markham, growth itself became an industry and some of Markham's foremost commercial realtors and developers got their starts. In 1967, when commercial and industrial development was not yet being seriously considered, Peter L. Mason Ltd.'s first transaction was a 50-acre parcel of land on the Ninth Line, ultimately donated for the site of the Markham-Stouffville Hospital. Since then the firm has been responsible for attracting many excellent corporate citizens such as the A.C. Nielsen Company of Canada Limited, located in the Milliken Mills Business Park, and has been instrumental in marketing most of the lands in the Town Centre Business Park at Warden and Highway 7.

Another commercial realtor, Carmen Di Paola, can also trace his company's success back to late 1960s. Having not yet started his own firm, Di Paola helped develop the first fully serviced industrial subdivision in the Denison Street/Woodbine area. MAI, one of the first computer companies to move to Markham, was among the firms that purchased land from him for a head office. For the next five years Di Paola, along with developers Vince Demarco and Rudy Bratty, played a major role in the continued development of the southern part of Markham.

Bratty's company, Cedarland Properties Limited, developed Milliken Mills Business Park. The development is situated on 300 acres and bordered by Steeles Avenue to the south,

Highway 7 to the north, Kennedy Road to the east, and Warden Avenue to the west. Some of Markham's largest and most prestigious corporate citizens are now located in this area, including IBM, American Express, and Apple Canada Inc.

IBM's relocation to Markham in 1982 is credited with turning the town into what has been called "Canada's Silicon Valley." In the wake of the computer giant came many other high-tech firms, both large and small. Newcomers in the last decade include Semi-Tech Microelectronics, Johnson Controls, GEAC Computers, Crowntek, Ford Electronics, Memorex, Hewlett-Packard, Mitsubishi Electric Sales Canada, Olivetti Canada, and a host of other companies that appear to arrive on a daily basis.

Although most of these companies are large enough to purchase land and construct their own corporate facilities, some smaller developments have been designed to specifically accommodate high-tech companies. The Apple Creek Centre is one such project. Located at Woodbine Avenue and McIntosh Drive, just north of Highway 7, it consists of three separate buildings totalling approximately 200,000 square feet of office and specialty space designed to fulfill a vast range of high-tech corporate needs. The headquarters of giant auto-parts manufacturer, Magna International, is also situated in this area.

Within walking distance of the Apple Creek development is the Valleywood Business Park and the headquarters of another Markham pacesetter. In 1986 Allstate Insurance Companies of Canada, an international insurer of life and property, moved into what has quickly become an architectural landmark. Its Canadian head office is a uniquely imposing 10-storey, black glass building. A central silo soars above two stepped wings and encloses a three-storey atrium.

Sharing the skyline with the Allstate building is Phase One of the Markham Corporate Campus, a spectacular five-storey building clad in rose-tinted, sculptured pre-cast concrete and reflective glass. This six-phase development will eventually total more than 900,000 square feet on 23 acres of parkland, with an on-site creek. It is owned by the Seltzer Organization, one of North America's most prestigious office park developers.

In the same business park is the Inducon Development Corporation's $125-million Valleywood Corporate Centre. This

ABOVE: Two-storey, Victorian-style brick residences stand in one of Markham's new residential developments. Photo by Glen Jones

LEFT: In the older residential areas of Markham, street signs such as these are a common sight. Photo by Pete Ryan. Courtesy, First Light

OPPOSITE: Some of Markham's youthful residents enjoy a stroll in the park. Photo by Glen Jones

project comprises four towers of reflective silver and blue glass, totalling 750,000 square feet of office space. When completed in the 1990s, the towers will be connected by a two-level office building that will serve as an all-weather link throughout the complex with a view of the natural park-like landscaping and an on-site, six-acre lake.

This Highway 404 corridor is a highly desirable business location and a number of other executive office complexes have been developed, such as the Gateway Centre at Steeles Avenue and the Parkway and York Corporate Centres at Highway 7. The latter project employs thousands of people in seven first-class office buildings, featuring restaurants, theatres, day-care, and other services on 34 acres.

President's Choice is another multi-tower complex located on 40 acres just south of Highway 7. The distinctive 10-storey Phase One Scotiabank Commercial Tower encompasses 168,500 square feet of office space and is sheathed in reflective silver and blue glass with aluminum panels. Designed by Inducon Consultants of Canada Limited, the building features a two-storey lobby finished in granite, mirrored glass, and stainless steel.

Two light industrial/commercial areas that are barely under development are further removed from the 404/7 transportation hub but just as accessible. They are the Town Centre Business Park at Warden Avenue and Highway 7 and, further south of Highway 7 between Woodbine Avenue and Highway 404, the 404 Business Park.

Surrounding the site of Markham's new civic centre, the Town Centre development is quickly erasing the last vestiges of rural life. One unusual project here is the Equity Town Centre, a three-phase complex which offers a limited partnership investment concept to professionals.

The Residences

While generating a large number of jobs, companies like these have, in turn, attracted a highly skilled and affluent population. The average income of Markham residents in 1983 was almost $25,000, compared to $17,300 for the general Canadian population.

But valued employees want more than paycheques.

Markham offers them homes of their own in a variety of settings—whether it's a turn-of-the-century frame house in a historic, tree-filled village; a country estate on rolling acres; a large and luxurious brick home in a carefully planned subdivision; or a state-of-the-art highrise or townhouse condominium.

Residential developers and builders have been kept busy as Markham's population swells toward an estimated 180,000 by the year 2000. The value of residential building permits in 1987 was almost $400 million, and housing was built at an average rate of 2,000 units per year during the last half of the 1980s.

From the old village where the first small subdivisions sprouted in the 1950s, the houses have pushed west toward Buttonville, filled in the space between Markham and Unionville, and taken over what was once farmland to the north. But nowhere is the sight of so many new homes as dramatic as in the south, along Steeles Avenue, in the new community of Milliken Mills.

Phase One of this massive development began in the late 1970s, when it was predicted that eventually the 350-acre town-within-a-town would have a population of 20,000. Now Milliken's projected population for the year 2001 is 59,000. Many of the houses are relatively small and affordable, at least compared to the statelier residences found in other parts of town. So many people in one area creates a need for new facilities, and planning has been carefully carried out to provide them. Land has been set aside for shopping centres, community recreation facilities, schools, senior citizens' housing, and libraries, which are materializing as the new residents settle into their homes.

In the older subdivisions of Markham, one can find winding lanes with comfortable, split-level dwellings on large lots, surrounded by lush landscaping. Newer streets are lined with larger and more imposing two-storey brick residences, like the unique, Victorian-style homes found in a luxurious development by Monarch Homes called the Bridle Trail.

Markham's housing stock also is well supplied with real Victoriana for those who prefer it to more modern architecture. Gingerbread trim, well-preserved clapboard, riotously colored gardens, and cool verandas invite the history lover to share in a living recognition of Markham's heritage and prosperity.

The British Toby gift shop specializes in "Royal Doulton and Collectible Cottages." Photo by

Dawn Goss. Courtesy, First Light

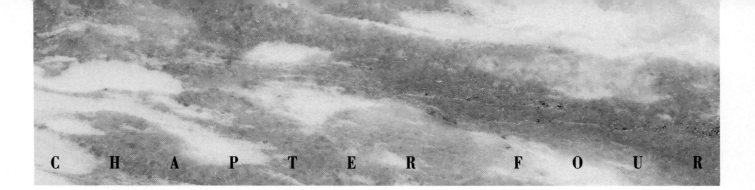

The Business of Service

Sitting on a park bench on Unionville's Main Street any Sunday afternoon in spring, one sees well-dressed shoppers and browsers sauntering leisurely along, waving greetings to friends and acquaintances.

In contrast, one has to hold onto one's hat on Main Street in Markham Village on a Friday morning, as cars and shoppers bustle from bank to grocery store and on down the street, finishing weekly chores.

Watching the traffic from the corner of Colborne and Yonge in Thornhill any day of the week, not all of it will be roaring by. Increasing numbers of shoppers are parking and discovering that the hometown businesses tucked into the nooks and crannies of the old village areas offer everything, and sometimes even more, than those in Toronto.

In these unique shopping areas that dot Markham's landscape, a variety of goods are sold from heritage buildings that have been lovingly cared for since a time when commerce was much simpler—when farmers bartered the fruits of their labors for a plow or other commodities that they could not produce themselves. In those days, a century ago, these buildings took their own individual places on the village streetscapes of Unionville, Thornhill, and Markham as homes, inns, blacksmith shops, and stables. As people rediscover the unique and special heritage of these areas, the structures have found second lives housing a variety of prosperous enterprises. And they stand proudly as precious evidence of Markham's history.

One such edifice, the Stiver House on Unionville's Main Street, is a perfect example of the wedding of business and historic home. Open the front door to this charming gift and craft shop and be ushered into a large formal entry hall, thought to have been used as a waiting room by the doctor who was the home's original occupant. Two fireplaces crackle their warmth on chilly days and an honest ambience, created by a century-and-a-half of living, welcomes visitors.

This building is distinctive because not only is it the oldest house remaining in the village, it is also the only remaining adobe brick structure. The "Ontario Cottage"-style, one-storey home was constructed around 1829. Although it was originally built for Dr. Thomas Eckardt, it has been continuously owned by the Stiver family for most of its history. The great-great-grandparents of the current owner purchased it in the 1870s, and subsequent generations of the family resided there until it was converted to a shop in the late 1970s.

Markham's Main Street has also seen a number of historic buildings converted for retail use in recent years. One of the most important and interesting of these was built in 1870 and is called the Wedding Cake House because of its ornate, white gingerbread trim. This picturesque building was home to the area's first car dealership in the 1920s and subsequently housed a tack shop, boutiques, and a tearoom. Under the ownership of a real estate firm, it has become the focal point of a heritage-style redevelopment project that includes both office and retail space.

Near the north end of the Main Street shopping area is the Wilson House, which has been given new life as a luxurious dining room. One can still walk up the veranda steps, through the front door, and into the home's gracious vestibule. Glass doors on one side open into the living room, and a grand staircase leads to a lounge. The yellow brick Victorian house was built in 1888 for a well-established general merchant in the village. In 1917 it was purchased by a doctor whose daughter maintained a practice there until she died in 1983.

The charm and economic viability of these unique retailing areas are nurtured by groups of merchants organized into municipally monitored organizations called Business Improvement Areas (BIAs). The BIAs organize street beautification schemes and mount advertising programs. Activities, conducted in conjunction with the Town of Markham, have included a $1.5-million beautification of Old Markham Village and a $1-million restoration of Unionville's downtown, both in the mid-1980s.

While these quaint shopping areas have prospered, they have gradually been supplemented by a variety of other retail establishments catering to Markham's growing and affluent population. Merchants find a ready market for their wares among residents who enjoy an average per capita yearly income that consistently ranks first or second in all of Canada. Retailing has become big business in the town and thousands of square feet of merchandising space are being added yearly. Today shoppers can purchase everything from groceries to luxury automobiles like BMWs right at home in Markham.

Complementing the interesting little village streetscapes are the service-oriented strip plazas that line Highway 7 as well as at least four major indoor shopping malls, with more being planned for the future. The largest and most elegant mall is Markville Shopping Centre. Opened in the early 1980s when that section of Highway 7 was still populated by the odd cow grazing in a farmer's field, the mall has become a landmark that covers almost 200 acres on the northwest corner of McCowan Road and Highway 7. The late 1980s saw a major expansion of Markville, which doubled its department stores to four and added many more specialty shops and services.

In the face of all this retail-sector growth, the commercial success of the village core areas has not been lost on developers. Taking their cue from the town's heritage shopping areas and encouraged by a caring municipal planning department and town council, developers have begun to build projects which

LEFT: Shoppers in Unionville peruse some wicker merchandise on display outdoors. Courtesy, Mel Reid & Associates

ABOVE: The Stiver House, a charming gift and craft shop located on Unionville's Main Street, was originally home to a doctor. Photo by Glen Jones

OPPOSITE: The 1870 Wedding Cake House, once home to the area's first car dealership and later used as a tack shop, boutique, and a tearoom, is now the focal point of a heritage-style redevelopment project including office and retail space. Photo by Jack Holman

retain the charm of the quaint streetscape but provide the benefits of the multi-unit shopping mall. The Markham Village Lanes and Town Hall projects, both on Markham's Main Street, are two such developments. But perhaps the most unique is a project on the town's southern border which has as its focus a startling complex of three barns with an 80-foot silo.

Built in 1983, Cullen Country Barns offers a unique mix of shopping and entertainment that attracts both local residents and tourists. Under the soaring barn roof, shoppers find a collection of boutiques that sell everything from women's and men's clothing to antiques, souvenirs, craft supplies, plants, gifts, and greeting cards. There is a country-style bakery and even a petting zoo. Four restaurants and a dinner theatre round out the Barns' offerings, making it no surprise that the expanding complex has received many national awards for entrepreneurship and retailing. Other developments furthering the country market theme have naturally located on properties adjacent to the Barns, broadening the retail opportunities even more.

Bed and Breakfast
The birth of Markham's business community and especially its hospitality industry can be traced to the nineteenth century,

Markville Shopping Centre, opened in the early 1980s and greatly expanded in the late 1980s, covers almost 200 acres and is Markham's largest and most elegant mall. Photo by Pete Ryan. Courtesy, First Light

when a large number of wayside taverns and town inns opened their doors to travellers. The often-impassable roads meant that inns—where travellers could eat, sleep, and tend to their horses—prospered. Tavern signs swung every mile or so along well-travelled roads. In 1858 there were 23 tavern owners licensed in Markham Township, and in the following years at least seven hotels along Yonge Street alone.

The taverns in turn encouraged more traffic, which meant that other businesses located nearby. Furthermore, the same poor roads that made life difficult for travellers made transportation of grain costly and led to the establishment, near the inns, of a variety of mills, distilleries, and breweries.

The taverns operated under a set of rules and regulations which decreed, among other things, that owners "must be ready at the shortest notice, to furnish a good and substantial breakfast, dinner or supper." The quality of the inns and the food they served varied widely. But they were social centres and the tavern owner was often the best known and most popular person in town.

The Queen's Hotel in Unionville, which still stands as one of the village's most picturesque buildings, was reportedly one of the better class of tavern. Mrs. John Webber, whose husband owned the hotel, was a fine cook, preparing gourmet meals on a huge wood-burning stove in the hotel kitchen. On special occasions she would begin a meal with oysters on the half-shell and carry right on through to charlotte russe accompanied by champagne—all for 50 cents.

Another, not so genteel, tavern was established at Milliken's Corners (along what is now Kennedy Road near the town's southern border). Its owner was Norman Milliken, a Loyalist settler from New Brunswick who established a lumbering business there in 1807. In order to control the drinking habits of his lumbermen, he opened the hotel under the management of his daughter, who was reportedly a large woman able to control any trouble that might arise.

Many of the tiny, local breweries were put out of business in the 1870s by the railway. And the mid-century temperance prohibitions, along with the construction of better roads, caused many other local distilleries and inns to close. The onset of the twentieth century and the development of the automo-

Upscale shops such as Mariani's Custom
Clothiers line Unionville's Main Street.
Courtesy, Mel Reid & Associates

bile took a further toll on these colorful establishments. The Queen's Hotel, for instance, was reduced to a boarding house with an attached snack bar until recent years, when it was renovated to house upscale boutiques and offices.

Nevertheless, fuelled by Markham's twentieth-century boom, the town's hospitality industry is again prospering. Since 1985 the town has experienced something of a hotel renaissance, with a number of new establishments locating near the Highway 404/7 core.

These are a far cry from the humble wayside stopovers of the previous century. They are first-class hotels, catering to both the corporate travellers who are increasingly visiting the area and the local business community.

The pioneer of these establishments was the Parkway Hotel. Located on the north side of Highway 7 just west of Highway 404, in what is now technically Richmond Hill, it was surrounded by rolling hills and fields when it opened in the early 1970s. In the 1980s the Sheraton chain pumped approximately $40 million into the low-rise motor hotel. The result was a two-towered facility that now serves the surrounding newly developed business community with a variety of first-class rooms, suites, and conference rooms.

Now called the Sheraton Parkway Hotel, it has developed a unique service that typifies the Markham hotel industry's determination to accomodate the business sector. In order to add to the comfort of the increasing number of executives from high-tech Japanese companies who stay at the hotel, a Japanese hospitality program has been established. The hotel hired a Japanese consultant to instruct its staff on that country's customs and language, and has made available a number of Japanese items including beer, foods, and newspapers.

Cullen Country Barns offers a unique mix of shopping and entertainment. Photo by Jack Holman

The 300-room Chimo Hotel, part of a Canadian-owned chain, also came to Markham in the mid-1980s. Located on Woodbine Avenue at Steeles, it, too, caters specifically to the business community with good conference and meeting facilities. But businesspeople are joined by local residents as they treat themselves to elegant gourmet dining in the hotel's renowned Berczy Room, named after the local settler and pioneer developer.

In addition to smaller chains like Signature Inn and Journey's End Motel, two major luxury hotel projects illustrate particularly well Markham's growing status in the Canadian business community.

The $25-million Valhalla Inn is part of the President's Choice office complex, just east of the Highway 404/7 intersection. With more than 200 rooms, complete dining and fitness facilities, and a variety of first-class meeting and convention

The 300-room Chimo Hotel on Woodbine Avenue at Steeles caters specifically to the business community with good conference and meeting facilities. Photo by Glen Jones

rooms, this Scandinavian-inspired hotel is the jewel in the Canadian company's crown.

Further along Highway 7, the green-tinted glass of the Markham Suites Hotel soars above the bustling Warden Avenue intersection like the wings of a majestic bird. The spectacular, 10-storey, all-suites atrium building is also home to Club Markham, a luxurious health club that is open to the public.

Markham's food-service sector has also matured over the past few decades. Those nineteenth-century away-from-home eateries were frequented mostly by men and were usually far from genteel in atmosphere. And even into the 1950s, eating out was not a particularly popular social or business pursuit. People who moved to Markham from more urban areas in the 1960s, and even in the early 1970s, found a small town with few places to eat and had to look to "the big city" for dining and entertainment.

But all that slowly began to change in the 1960s when the town's first fast-food franchise opened its doors, and local families were able to join people all across the continent in responding to the advertising slogan, "Let's All Go to the Dairy Queen."

From fast food to traditional dining, all styles of restaurants have taken their places in modern Markham. Residents and visitors can now satisfy any culinary desire from steak, pizza, seafood, or desserts to nouvelle cuisine, sandwiches, oriental food, or a variety of other ethnic fare. And during warm weather, the three village centres are dotted with colorful umbrellas as casual diners leisurely watch life go by from outdoor patios.

Markham also has its share of gracious, formal dining

rooms of the type where mom and dad celebrate their anniversaries with roast beef dinners and important business deals are closed. Given that the area is so blessed with grand old homes and heritage buildings, it was inevitable that a good number of them would be turned into this type of elegant restaurant.

Supplementing these restaurants and the hotel dining rooms is perhaps the pinnacle of the eating-as-celebration trend: Le Parc, a massive and well-appointed banquet and convention centre that can accommodate 2,000 people. The popular facility, located across from the Sheraton Parkway Hotel, can host weddings with anywhere from 80 to 1,200 guests.

Professional Service

Along with the hospitality industry, many service and profes-

sional businesses have located in Markham since its urbanization began.

If sound financial institutions are the backbone of a healthy economy, Markham's cheeks must be rosy indeed. In fact, the casual observer might think that the venerable Bay Street financial district of Toronto is about to move lock, stock, and barrel to Markham!

The major players in the Canadian banking community —the Bank of Nova Scotia, the Royal Bank, the Canadian Imperial Bank of Commerce, the Bank of Montreal, and the Toronto Dominion Bank—all have established commercial banking centres in the Highway 404/7 area.

And along with the banks come a variety of related professionals, like accounting and legal firms, so that both the corporate sector and the individual investor can be provided with a full range of services.

Other members of the Markham financial community are American Express and A.C. Nielsen Company, both of which have their Canadian headquarters in Milliken Mills. In addition, two of the country's largest banks—Scotia Bank and the Commerce—have located their electronic data centres there.

OPPOSITE: Standing on Highway 7 and Warden Avenue is the spectacular Markham Suites Hotel. Courtesy, Mel Reid & Associates

ABOVE: Classicomm Communications is the cable television station serving Markham. Photo by Jack Holman

Keeping in Touch

The art of communication has become a sophisticated, technologically based pursuit. But in Markham's early days, communication was confined primarily to word of mouth. The first signs of pioneer settlement—land cleared, cabins built—sparked a

A family enjoys an ice cream break on Unionville's Main Street. Photo by Dawn Goss. Courtesy, First Light

desire for a better means of communication.

And sure enough, in 1827, just a few decades after the first settlers came to Markham, the first newspaper appeared. The *Farmers' Gazette,* which only lasted a few years, was followed by the *Markham Advertiser,* which also had a short life.

In 1856 a public-spirited politician named David Reesor founded the *Economist,* a paper that proclaimed itself to be "a journal of strong Reform proclivities." A rival paper—both in circulation and politics—named the *Sun* was started by local Tory George Chauncey in 1881. The two papers survived side by side until 1915 when the *Economist* bought the *Sun,* creating the *Economist and Sun.* The paper, now part of the huge Metroland printing and publishing conglomerate which publishes the *Toronto Star* as well as many suburban weeklies, has flourished. In 1988 it increased its frequency from one paper a week to three.

Because Markham is so close to Toronto, a city that has four major daily newspapers and a large number of television and radio stations, its residents enjoy access to a wide variety of media. But since the advent of that first primitive paper in 1827, the lively art of communication has also been well represented locally.

The cable television station that serves Markham, Classicomm Communications Ltd., provides a wide variety of local programming as well as access to most of the popular national and American commercial and pay-TV networks. In 1987 the company became the first in Canada to offer a special selection of cable television packages to businesses by specially wiring the Esna Park Business Park, near Steeles and Woodbine, and the 404 Business Park, near Highway 7.

With Markham's high income level, strong retail sector,

and large number of new businesses providing a lucrative advertising market, a variety of controlled-circulation publications flourish. There are many consumer magazines published for and delivered to Markham residents. And business-to-business publishing is equally successful, with a large number of companies producing periodicals and directories. Local businesses have their own communications vehicle, the *Markham/York Region Business Journal,* a privately published monthly newspaper founded in 1987.

The craft of printing such publications has come a long way since the days when David Reesor cranked out the *Economist* on a hand press. And Markham's host of modern printing companies utilizes every technological improvement to provide a wide variety of services to the business community, from advertising specialties, business forms, and container labels to books and credit cards.

In fact, Markham is becoming something of a graphic arts centre—home to a remarkable number of graphic arts firms, advertising agencies, and public relations firms, some with large national accounts.

The diversity and quality of these communications industries indicate, once again, that Markham has emerged as a sophisticated leader in the country's business community.

The 1829 Stiver House is the only remaining adobe brick structure in Unionville and the village's oldest house. Photo by Glen Jones

A railroad car stands idle on the tracks at the Heritage Museum. Photo by Pete Ryan.

Maintaining the Heritage

Much of Markham's strength can be credited to the souls of its founders. The determination and courage of William Berczy's German settlers, as well as of the French Royalists and Pennsylvania Dutch who followed, shaped the township's early development. The cultures and customs of these European pioneers left an indelible mark on life in Markham, a life to which many of the pioneers' descendants still contribute.

Now, almost 200 years later, people of many other nationalities have come to settle in Markham and add their own distinctive cultures to those established in 1793. The town's face has been transformed into a modern multicultural mosaic.

Thornhill is home to a strong concentration of Jewish families, while a veritable United Nations of ethnic groups is scattered throughout the rest of the town. The multicultural flavor is especially strong in Milliken Mills, the newly developed community that stretches across the town's southern border. More than 40 languages have been identified as being spoken in that area alone,

ABOVE: Visitors to the Markham District Historical Museum can tour an 1824 Mennonite log cabin. Photo by Pete Ryan. Courtesy, First Light

OPPOSITE: The Locust Hill Canadian Pacific Railway station now stands as a part of the Historical Museum. Photo by Pete Ryan. Courtesy, First Light

with only 21 percent of its residents having been born in Canada. Among the rest are people from Western Europe, the Caribbean, India, Italy, Greece, and Asia, especially Hong Kong.

Respect for the differences of other cultures is being fostered within the community in a variety of ways. Multicultural activities such as exchange programs and festivals are often highlights of the academic year for local schoolchildren. Even the littlest citizens become involved in weaving the unique Markham tapestry: one Milliken day-care centre, with an enrolment reflecting more than 30 nationalities, regularly organizes multicultural activities.

The Markham Council is also in tune with the fact that the make-up of the community has changed during the past few decades. Through its Multicultural Association and Committee On Race And Ethno-Cultural Equity, it assists in enhancing harmonious relations among ethnic groups.

Inspired by the Past

To their continuing credit, all of Markham's residents realize that their community's heritage is the source of its charm. This consciousness is typified by the strong community support of its museum.

Situated on 22 acres on Highway 48 north of the village of Markham, the Markham District Historical Museum is one of southern Ontario's largest community museums. It was opened in 1970 through the efforts of local historian and sixth-generation Markhamite John W. Lunau, with the assistance of the local Lions Club.

Thanks to Lunau, who also founded the Markham District Historical Society, visitors can trace the town's origins and experience a slice of its history. The museum's main building is the former Mount Joy Public School, an imposing brick edifice built in 1907. It houses three galleries of artifacts from the past as well as the municipal archives. In addition to a room in a typical pioneer home, there is a dentist's office, a cobbler's working area, a harness maker's equipment, and a general store. In the place of honor is a plough, the symbol of the thousands of hours of back-breaking labor that shaped the township.

During the summer visitors can tour the museum's other buildings, guided by university students. These buildings include an 1824 Mennonite home; the oldest church in Markham, dating back to 1848; a diesel-powered sawmill; a stream-driven cider mill; a CP railway station from Locust Hill; and the Acadia, a government rail car used by five prime minis-

BELOW: This railroad car is on display at the Historical Museum. Photo by Pete Ryan. Courtesy, First Light

OPPOSITE: A new home constructed in the "old style" stands in a heritage-conscious section of Unionville. Courtesy, Mel Reid & Associates

ters. They can also enjoy two large special collections of horse-drawn vehicles and agricultural implements.

The museum hosts some very special events of interest to locals and visitors alike. Founder's Day in June celebrates the life skills that the first settlers needed to survive in the hostile countryside. Visitors on that day are encouraged to plough a furrow with a team of Belgian horses, much as Markham's founders did hundreds of years ago. There is also Heritage Day in September, sponsored by the Markham Historical Society. This traditional post-harvest celebration features demonstrations, music, entertainment, and fine food. Applefest, held in October, is a nineteenth-century celebration commemorating the apple harvest. It features old-time, hand-powered methods of peeling, pressing, and cooling apples at the museum's cider mill.

Community support for this museum is substantial. The local government pays a large part of its operating costs, the Lions Club has undertaken construction projects on the site, and even the Markham Horticultural Society pitches in, supplying the grounds with traditional flowers and greenery.

Living History
However, in Markham, respect for heritage means much more than preserving the past behind the fences and walls of a museum. In Markham, history lives.

It lives in a unique heritage subdivision located just outside the museum's boundaries. This exciting 40-lot project is home to a growing number of heritage homes that have been plucked from the jaws of destruction. Under an unusual solution to the conflicting needs of preservationists and developers, families can purchase a designated heritage home and transplant it into the subdivision. The town maintains architectural control over the community and spent close to $2 million to service it in 1988, while owners restore the homes and reside in them.

History also lives in the old village centres of Markham, Unionville, Thornhill, and Buttonville, where preservation and careful development have been spearheaded by individuals as well as groups of community-minded residents. Concerned —and where necessary, militant—ratepayer groups have a tradition of eloquently and often effectively fighting to maintain the

OPPOSITE, TOP: The Queen's Hotel, a landmark building in the village of Unionville, was purchased and restored by local families. Photo by Glen Jones

OPPOSITE, BOTTOM: Several old homes may be found in Markham, Unionville, and Thornhill. Courtesy, Mel Reid & Associates

RIGHT: Funseekers test their luck and skill at "pig racing" at the Markham Fair. Courtesy, Mel Reid & Associates

ABOVE: Dressed in splendid theatrical attire, an organist performs at the Markham Agricultural Fair. Photo by Pete Ryan. Courtesy, First Light

quality of life in their town. And many developers are slowly but surely taking on the refreshing attitude of restoration and rehabilitation rather than razing.

As well, active community historical societies are ever-poised to protect precious heritage buildings. Their volunteer work is supported and facilitated by the town's Heritage Coordinator and Heritage Markham, a local architectural conservation advisory committee. Established under the Ontario Heritage Act, Heritage Markham's mandate is to ensure that the town's historic buildings are not lost to development.

Under the same provincial legislation, the old villages of Markham, Unionville, and Thornhill have been given special heritage designations. Depending on the type of designation, development within designated sections of these villages is subject to stringent controls or at least heritage consideration. Neighbourhood compatibility is one particularly important criterion, made to ensure that Markham preserves its special ambience.

The Society for the Preservation of Thornhill is another community group that has been instrumental in saving properties of historical significance. It was formed in the 1970s in response to residents' concern over what they saw as the homogenizing influences and excesses of wholesale land development in the popular Yonge Street corridor. Their vigilance has been effective; close to 100 historic buildings still stand in that village as reminders of the past.

Similarly, the Old Markham Village Preservation Society was formed in 1986 to fight for the preservation of an 1872-vintage hotel building on the village's Main Street. The building's developer, who had concluded it was too expensive to restore the structure to modern building code standards for commer-

cial use, was thwarted by the group in his plans to demolish it and build a replica on the site.

Decades earlier, a landmark hotel in Unionville village was also preserved through the efforts of local citizens. The Queen's Hotel was purchased and restored by local families after the previous owner sought demolition and a leading restoration architect declared it was not economically feasible to save.

In fact, concern for the protection of Markham's heritage is nowhere more obvious than in Unionville, where the story of the residents' fight to protect their village has become a local legend. The saga begins with a meeting of neighbours that took place in a church basement in 1968, a meeting that was to change the course of history in the village that calls itself "The Antique Capital of Ontario."

The community's first major subdivision was just being

planned, and eager families were discovering that Unionville's suburban tranquility was a good place to escape the urbanization of Metropolitan Toronto. Caught up in the development fervor, the township council decided to widen the village's Main Street to four lanes, a project that would require the removal of some of its 30-odd pioneer buildings and an ancient tree or two.

Alarmed that their lovely old village would become a dusty, noisy truck run, the residents of Unionville determined to fight for their quality of life. Grouped together under the banner of the Unionville Conservation and Development Association, they decided to hold a festival to convince the world of the value of maintaining their architectural jewels. The festival, held in June 1970, succeeded beyond the organizing committee's wildest dreams, with thousands of people attending. The subsequent wide media coverage and public outcry saved the village, and a by-pass was built around it.

This was the impetus needed to make the village one of the most popular tourist and shopping attractions in southern Ontario. Buildings were spruced up, additions were carefully constructed, and new retailers gradually joined the antique dealers who had already discovered the street's charm.

The rejuvenation was completed almost two decades later when utility wires, hanging like old clotheslines, were buried out of sight. Brick paving, reproduction lampposts, park benches, and hanging flower baskets were also added during the facelift.

Celebrating the Past
The festival that started it all has endured. The three-day Unionville Village Festival is a very successful and pleasurable annual event, organized by a residents' committee that works hard to ensure that things run smoothly and the small-town flavor remains. Tens of thousands of people, from Markham and across the province, gather in the street in the sunshine (it never dares rain), participating in the many free activities and listening to the strolling entertainment. A marathon race, a Sunday family picnic in the park, and a nostalgia dance on Friday evening round out the weekend's activities.

But this type of event, which evokes a strong community

spirit, is not unique to Unionville. Throughout town, annual village festivals provide a meeting place for both new and established residents. Markham Village's Main Street is the site of its own festival, held each year in June. And while the skies may be grey overhead, the annual Santa Claus Parade, organized by the Kinsmen Club, brightens the faces of children and adults alike as it passes along Main Street in late November.

In the town's new southern community of Milliken Mills, Summerfest, which is organized annually by the local community association, reflects that area's multicultural character.

And every year in September, the Thornhill Village Festival takes visitors on a journey back to the 1800s through activities such as a parade of antique cars, floats, and marching bands, and crafts and homemade foods. Visitors dressed in period costumes are admitted to the grounds free, and a contest is held to judge the best outfits.

Perhaps the biggest festival of all, and certainly the one that most directly communicates Markham's roots, is the Agricultural Fair held each fall. Organized by the Markham and East York Agricultural Society, it is one of the largest annual rural fairs held in Ontario.

It is a traditional country fair, bringing a bit of country to the suburbs, complete with home baking and needlework competitions, tractor pulls, and livestock shows. In 1977 the fairgrounds, a collection of buildings constructed on 100 acres in rural north Markham, replaced the original township fairgrounds located at the corner of highways 7 and 48 at the busy south end of Markham Village's Main Street.

Proving time and time again that community spirit is alive and well in Markham, hundreds of energetic residents volunteer large amounts of time and energy to help make the fair and other community events successful.

Many others leave their own unique legacies to the town, building, piece by piece, the multicolored mosaic that is modern Markham. One such person was early resident William Fleming, who died in 1905. Fleming held the title of Champion Draughtsplayer of Canada from 1868 to 1890. On the checker champion's gravestone in St. Andrew's Presbyterian Cemetery sits a full-sized checkerboard on a granite pedestal, a lasting testimonial to his skill and, perhaps, to his sense of humor.

Fitness is becoming a way of life for Markham's energetic residents. Photo by Glen Jones

Nurturing Body and Soul

Markham is a drawing card for those who value a home and a special way of life. But a lifestyle involves more than a place called home. Today's energetic families want much more than just paycheques—they want things to do and places to do them. So it is that up-to-the-minute fitness centres, well-maintained parks and conservation areas, playing fields, arenas, pools, community centres and libraries with a wealth of planned activities, art galleries, and theatre facilities are all part of modern Markham.

Leisure activities have always played a key role in defining the character of the town and its people. In Markham's very early days, its pioneers could not afford to spend time on aimless pursuits; everything they did had a purpose. From baking bread to curing meat and churning butter, from sewing intricately detailed quilts and weaving woollen cloth to building wooden dowry chests and other furniture, simplicity and economy marked the fruits of their labors.

Because pioneer life was so difficult, the pleasures of local taverns provided a welcome respite. Farmers also consumed a great deal of liquid refreshment at events which combined hard work with recreation, such as logging bees and barn raisings and at harvest time. The inevitable abuse of all this liquor led to the wave of temperance that swept through North America—and Markham—in the mid-1800s. Almost every village in the township eventually had a Temperance Hall, where temperance tea parties and dances were held on a regular basis.

The churches were also the focus of community social life. One account describes an event put on by St. Andrew's Wesleyan Methodist Church which, true to the work ethic, was held for the purpose of raising money for the reconstruction of the church building. The ladies of the church held a bazaar in the town hall, which they decorated with evergreens and flowers. The dining tables groaned under the weight of meat, vegetables, and an endless variety of cookies, cakes, and pies. Following the dinner, there was musical entertainment and speeches.

As the decades passed, life became easier and people developed other interests to fill their increasing spare time. Ironically, some of those rigorous pioneer activities are now being pursued as hobbies, as modern Markhamites make an effort to get back in touch with basic, country-style values.

In modern Markham, life is good and spare time is abundant, and the diversity of leisure activities has never been greater. The number of recreational facilities and programs is continually increasing to keep up with the pace of growth in the town. Between 1979 and 1988, the Town of Markham spent more than $50 million on new and upgraded libraries, recreation centres and parks, and other facilities.

Focus for the Arts

One of the major capital projects was the Markham Theatre for Performing Arts. This superb, $5-million showcase has provided a focal point for the town's vibrant performing and visual arts. Located at the corner of Warden Avenue and Highway 7, it was built as the first stage of the town's Civic Centre complex and now shares the site with the municipal offices.

When it opened, it represented a new stage of cultural awareness in the town. The intimate and elegant state-of-the-art performance centre, for which the community's cultural leaders had long been hungering, was a major step forward. On opening night in October 1985, only hours after construction workers had applied the finishing touches, every one of its 528 seats was filled. The well-equipped hall rang with the sounds of famous Canadian jazz musicians Moe Koffman, Guido Basso, and Rob McConnell. From that first memorable show, the theatre has evolved into the largest variety presenter of professional subscription events in Canada, with an eclectic mix of professional Canadian and international talent from the National Ballet of Canada to opera singer Maureen Forrester and world-famous mime Marcel Marceau.

Besides bringing big-name professional performers to town, the theatre has provided an important focus for the local performing arts community. It devotes time and space to local youth by opening its doors to area school groups for musical and drama performances. Holding the inside track is Unionville High School, attached to the theatre by a walkway. The school makes good use of the theatre during the time available and has thus developed a strong performing arts program.

In a mutually responsive relationship, the theatre has benefited from community input. Its board of management is made up of residents from across the town as well as politicians. Besides playing a contributing role in programming and marketing decisions, the board has also been active in fund-raising for the theatre's development and promotion of the arts.

Community of Creativity
The theatre complements a wide variety of other cultural activities that take place, which fulfill residents' need for both recreation and creativity. Whether a person is interested in sculpting, painting, singing, dancing, or playing an instrument, he or she is likely to find some soul mates among Markham's talented residents. The Cachet Choral Group, Cantabile Chorale, Scottish Country Dancers, York Symphony, Markham Men of Harmony, Markham Concert Band, Village Harmonizers, York Choraliers, and the York Symphony Orchestra are just some of the groups which allow Markhamites to come together to pursue and share their talents.

These groups are part of a long local tradition of talented people making music together. The town's archives contain

turn-of-the-century photographs of the solemn-faced members of the Markham Village Brass Band, the Cedar Grove Youth Choir, and the Markham Dramatic Club and Orchestra.

While the origins of Markham Little Theatre do not go back quite so far, it is still one of the oldest cultural groups in the town. The success of this enthusiastic theatre company —founded in 1966—can be measured not only in terms of the tears and laughter generated by its participants, but in awards won. The theatre's original members, some of whom still play important roles, first rehearsed in the agricultural building at the old fairgrounds. Cold temperatures and uncomfortable conditions resulted in their moving rehearsals to the basements of various members' homes. But the budding thespians soon required larger quarters, and the group eventually moved into a suite of rooms above the old Town Cinema on Markham Village's Main Street.

This was better, but not exactly ideal: if a movie was being shown, rehearsing actors had to whisper their lines even when a screech was more appropriate. Set pieces, props, costumes, and lights had to be lowered by block and tackle from an open window to a truck waiting below to deliver them to the sparse auditorium at Markham District High School, where performances

LEFT: One of Markham's senior artists puts brush to canvas to paint a picture of a lovely house. Photo by Glen Jones

were held. Needless to say, the advent of the Markham Theatre was particularly welcomed by this group, although rehearsal, set-building, and storage space is still at a premium for what ranks as one of Ontario's best community theatre groups.

The talents of visual artists are also well nurtured. The Markham Group of Artists and Thornhill Village Artists both have many accomplished painters among their numbers and hold regular shows of members' work. This is not surprising given the place that painters hold in Markham's history. At various times, five members of the famous Group of Seven painters lived in Thornhill, and member Fred Varley resided on Unionville's Main Street during the 1950s and 1960s. The historic Salem Eckardt House, where Varley stayed with the McKay family, has been donated to the town for a public gallery along with a collection of his work. There are also a variety of private, commercial galleries in the town, offering for sale works of many different styles.

BELOW: Step dancers perform on Main Street. Courtesy, Mel Reid & Associates

Libraries are another source of culture and learning that is taken seriously in Markham. The town spent $4.3 million on library construction in 1987 and 1988. Four branches house more than 200,000 circulating books as well as

magazines, newspapers, business and government reports, records, cassettes, films, movie screens, projectors, and video cassettes and recorders. They also offer courses on microcomputers and crafts as well as children's reading programs, "moms and tots" activities, and story times.

Markham's sense of history is also evident through its library system. The Thornhill Village Library is a charming and unique branch housed in a pre-Confederation house, restored in 1977 by the Markham Public Library Board, the town, and local citizens. Situated on a quiet street in the Thornhill Heritage Conservation District, the branch is a focal point for the people of the old village, but is also used by residents from other parts of the town who enjoy its sense of history and community.

Recreation

One of Markham's earliest sports facilities was built for the Markham Fair in the 1890s. An impressive wood-and-brick structure with a curved roof, it was used by the community for ice-skating and curling until it was destroyed by fire in 1916.

Today the town's Parks and Recreation Department oversees the mammoth task of creating and maintaining a variety of parks and recreational facilities, as well as programs, for residents of all ages. The people who live and work in Markham enjoy a wealth of green spaces: in 1988, there were more than 125 parks—community parks with major playing fields and play equipment, as well as smaller "parkettes" designed with tots in mind.

Outdoor sports facilities are also plentiful. Many of the town's baseball diamonds are lit for night play, as are some of its soccer fields. There are close to 40 tennis courts and an equal number of ice surfaces. As well as two beaches, there are a variety of walking and fitness trails (in existence and planned), which span over 10 kilometres. In addition, two ponds are groomed during the winter for pleasure skating and hockey.

The indoor facilities are equally extensive and, like everything offered by the town, they are always increasing in number to keep up with residential growth. In 1987 there were six town-operated community centres, which together incorporated seven artificial ice surfaces, two fitness centres, five squash courts, indoor and outdoor running tracks, and two indoor swimming pools.

The town offers fitness programs in two comprehensively equipped gymnasiums. At the Markham Fitness Centres, located in community centres on John Street and Bayview in Thornhill and McCowan north of Highway 7 in Unionville, these facilities employ fully qualified staff who design individual fitness programs and coordinate organized exercise classes.

A few outdoor facilities also deserve special mention. Milne Park, more than 300 acres of conservation land leased from the area conservation authority, features lots of wide-open space as well as picnic grounds and barbecue facilities.

Unionville's Toogood Pond is another special recreational facility. The pond, a section of the Rouge River system that has been dammed up to control spring flooding, has been slowly civilized over the years. Picnic areas and manicured walking trails were created around the pond but haven't disturbed the habitat of resident wildlife, which includes Canada geese and mallard ducks. Residents can canoe on the pond in summer and skate on it in winter, thanks to the care of Markham Parks and Recreation.

Just steps from Unionville's historic Main Street, the pond has become a focal point for a subdivision of luxury homes. But it has long been used as a recreational facility by residents —although not without hazards. In fact, the Unionville Swimming Club had its origins in the 1950s when residents decided to negotiate with the property's owner, Art Toogood, in an attempt to decrease the frequency of accidents in the pond area.

Aside from maintaining these facilities, the Parks and Recreation Department organizes programs for all ages at locations in neighbourhoods across town. For preschoolers, the recreation centres offer activities with descriptive names like "Babygym," "Clay Play," "Kindergym," "Rainbows and Rhythm," and "Tiny Tumblers." For school-aged children, there are programs that include skill development training in such pursuits as ballet and jazz dance, skating, pottery, archery, basketball, karate, and cooking. For adults, there's aerobics, badminton, fencing, self-defence, ballroom dancing, microwave and gourmet cooking, calligraphy, crafts, and much more.

But these programs do not outshine the department's traditional mainstay and one of the best methods of keeping fit: swimming. Instructional courses and recreational swims are scheduled for all ages at the town's two indoor pools. Red Cross and Royal Lifesaving programs are offered in addition to everything from basic swimming lessons for preschoolers through adults to competitive swimming programs. Professional Aquatics Development courses, which train professional aquatic instructors and lifeguards, are also available.

All these activities are described in quarterly guidebooks published by the Parks and Recreation Department, circulated to each household in the town. Registration is by mail or in person on specified registration days, and an attempt is made to involve all community members in the various programs. Senior citizens, for instance, may register in any adult program for half of the regular registration fee. Baby-sitting is offered for many programs, and individuals with special needs or handicaps are integrated into programs whenever possible.

In addition to all the regularly scheduled activities, indoor ice rinks, pools, and lifeguards can be rented by residents for special events like birthday parties and family reunions. The community centres also rent out their meeting rooms. These

ABOVE: Parkettes, such as this one on Varley Drive, account for some of the more than 125 parks in Markham. Photo by Winston Fraser

OPPOSITE: The Town of Markham spent more than $4 million on library construction in 1987 and 1988. Four branches, including the one shown here, house more than 200,000 circulating books as well as magazines, newspapers, records, films, and more. Photo by Winston Fraser

OPPOSITE, TOP: Hockey players can take to the ice at any of three skating arenas in the Markham area. Photo by Glen Jones

OPPOSITE, BOTTOM: There are a variety of fitness and walking trails spanning more than 10 kilometres in Markham. Photo by Glen Jones

range from an intimate lounge suitable for weddings and other social events to a boardroom with kitchen facilities, a room equipped with dance barres and mirrors, conference rooms with lecterns and microphones, and community banquet halls.

In addition to the programs run by the Parks and Recreation Department, more than 50 sports clubs and special interest athletic organizations—catering to both adults and children—bring their own lively activities to the local recreation scene. Many of them use town facilities.

Team sports are very popular, and leagues prosper in most sports. In winter, hockey is king, led by the Markham Waxers Jr. B Hockey Club, which plays bruising home games at Centennial Arena.

The Markham, Unionville, and Thornhill minor hockey associations have teams for children of all ages; their dads play in the Men's Recreational Hockey League. Adults who prefer the more civilized winter sport of curling can belong to the Curling Club of Unionville, which boasts its own facility and has hosted international competitions. And while some parents get up before dawn on cold winter mornings to drive their children to hockey practice, others are bound for figure skating. Clubs at all three village arenas have honed some very successful talent and sponsor yearly skating extravaganzas.

Summer brings a move outdoors, and Markham's ball diamonds are kept busy by close to two dozen leagues. Slow pitch is especially popular, but it is being challenged by the sport of soccer, which attracts more players every year. In 1988 the Thornhill Soccer Club had more than 1,000 participants in that part of town alone, from five-year-olds to seniors. Five hundred youngsters played in the Mini program, 300 in the House League, and 200 in a Rep Competitive program which has won three cup finals and two league championships since 1987. The Markham/Unionville equivalents, Markham Youth Soccer and Markham Senior Soccer, are equally as popular, and more clubs are being formed all the time.

Tennis, with a dozen clubs, and swimming are very popular non-team sports. A variety of swim clubs operate out of the town's two public pools. These include the Markham Aquatic Club, which is authorized by the Canadian Amateur Swimming Association, and the Synchronized Swimming Club.

Markham is also home to at least three gymnastics clubs, two of which have their own custom-built facilities. Both the Markham Gymnastics Club and the Winstonettes Gymnastics Club offer excellent instructors and programs, as does the Kalev Estienne Markham Rhythmic Gymnastics Centre, which runs a more limited but specialized program in a school gymnasium.

Other popular organized sports include basketball, bowling (both indoor and lawn bowling), cricket, cycling, football, judo, lacrosse, ringette, rugby, running, and volleyball.

Ever in pursuit of good health and the perfect body, a high percentage of Markhamites belong to private fitness clubs. These range from the posh and state-of-the-art Club Markham at the Markham Suites Hotel to those offering basic, no-frills muscle building.

Since, traditionally, a great deal of business has been conducted on the golf course, it is natural that such facilities are popular in corporate-minded Markham. There are at least five private or public golf courses within the town's boundaries and an equal number just outside.

THIS PAGE: Area residents can enjoy a variety of peaceful activities at Markham's Toogood Pond. (Top & right) Photos by Pete Ryan. Courtesy, First Light (Above) Courtesy, Mel Reid & Associates

With this great wealth of athletic facilities and programs, it is easy to see how Markham has produced its share of world-class athletes, including the 1988 Canadian parachuting champion, several international gymnastic champions, and the 1964 Olympic silver medal winner in the 800-metre track event.

For those whose interests lie in areas other than sports, the Markham Guild of Village Crafts offers programs which provide opportunities to explore and learn a variety of crafts. Members attend monthly general meetings and offer courses in such handiwork as quilting, knitting, smocking, spinning, pottery, weaving, and rug hooking.

Although the business community profits well by feeding the hunger that Markham residents have for sports and leisure activities, its involvement doesn't stop at profit generation. The cornucopia of available non-profit facilities and events is dependent upon the support of local businesses. Markham companies offer a high level of sponsorship for cultural, civic, sports, and social projects, both large and small. These range from the sponsorship of Markham Theatre subscription events by corporations like Allstate and American Express to a restaurant's anonymous donation of food for an amateur theatre rehearsal to the provision of sweaters for a minor-league hockey team by real estate salespeople. This community service ethic has become woven into the fabric of Markham, and is what makes Markham such a friendly—and all around healthy—place to live.

German Lutherans constructed Bethesda Church in Unionville Village in 1862.

Photo by Glen Jones

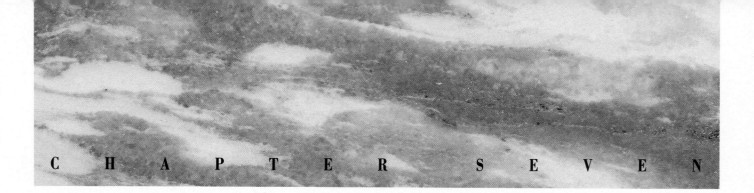

A Legacy of
Caring and Sharing

Traditionally, one of the main networks linking various parts of a community has been its school system. And that is certainly the case in Markham. Its two publicly funded school systems—the York Region Roman Catholic Separate School Board and the York Region Board of Education—provide not only quality education but also a focus for community activities.

Since Markham's early residents, who arrived after William Berczy in the 1700s, were largely German, the area's earliest schools were likely conducted in that language. But one of the earliest recorded accounts of Markham Township schools is in the *Legislative Journal* for March 1835. John Crosby and six other men are recorded as petitioning the central government for money to furnish a red brick school they had built north of Markham Village to accommodate 50 to 60 young elementary students.

By 1837 there was a demand for higher education in the village, and the Markham Village

101

Unionville High School, connected with the Markham Theatre for the Performing Arts, is home to an innovative, intensive arts program called Arts York. Photo by Glen Jones

Grammar School was constructed. In 1871 it became a high school, and students from as far away as Stouffville and Agincourt travelled there each day by train. The frame structure was replaced by a more substantial brick building in 1879, a structure that formed the nucleus for the elementary school that presently occupies the same site.

Another early education story tells how students attending the Thornhill School had to carry in wood each winter morning to fire up the wood stoves. Since there was no heat at night, the ink bottles would freeze. Boys being boys, they would collect the bottles and set them on top of the box stove, where inevitably some would explode and spray the ceiling with ink.

More recent school board history is sprinkled wih stories about coping with the ever-increasing numbers of new students moving to the area. A 1945 newspaper article described a report by an inspector who had toured Markham High School. He reported that the building was inadequate in size and lacked a gymnasium, auditorium, library, lunchroom, dressing room facilities, and space for shop work and home economics. The school, now called Markham District High School, eventually received all of those facilities and more, growing to accommodate close to 2,000 students. For a long time it was Markham's only public high school east of Bayview Avenue, but by the late 1980s the huge increase in population had necessitated the openings of three new public high schools.

Educating for the Future
The York Region Board of Education has a policy of designating its high schools as specialists in specific areas of study. The Milliken Mills High School, for instance, opened in 1989 to accommodate that fast-growing community, has a science bias in addition to its regular academic program. The newest, Quantztown High School, has been named after a pioneer settlement that was located nearby, at the intersection of 16th Avenue and McCowan Road.

Meanwhile, the halls of Unionville High School resound with the melodic but monotonous sound of musical scales. In a spacious, window-lined room, artworks-in-progress sit alongside sculpture armatures, drawing boards, and pottery wheels. Around the corner, another room is equipped with a wooden floor, mirrors, and ballet barres. And downstairs in the drama room, one might typically find 20 teenagers sitting on the carpeted floor, running through lines from Shakespeare's *Twelfth Night*.

This school, which is attached to the Markham Theatre for Performing Arts, is home to an innovative, intensive arts program called Arts York. Young people, not only from Markham but from the whole York Region, audition each year for the 100 new grade-nine places in the program. Students carry a full academic load as well as attending specialized classes in visual arts,

The demand for day-care in Markham is far outstripping the supply, and waiting lists are common. Photo by Dawn Goss. Courtesy, First Light

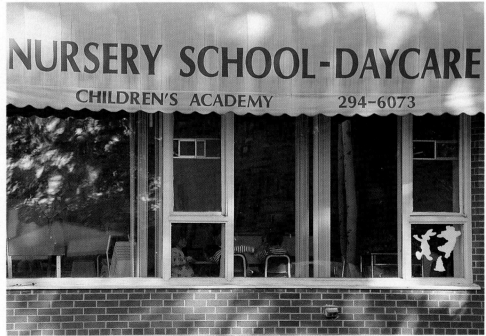

Magna International Inc. has a Technical Training Centre designed to help fulfill the company's need for skilled tool and die makers and other technicians. Photo by Pete Ryan. Courtesy, First Light

theatre, dance, or music. Visiting professional artists supplement the instruction given by qualified teachers in specially designed facilities for each subject major.

Other secondary school students, who are focused on careers in the business world, have the opportunity to participate in a Co-operative Education program. This is the fastest-growing form of education locally, allowing hundreds of high school students to gain on-the-job experience that may be a stepping stone to a future career. Under the supervision of an employer and the monitoring of their Co-operative Education teacher, participating students are confronted with reality that gives relevance to their traditional in-school education.

The local businesses who sponsor Co-operative Education students join the caretakers who organize fishing derbies for handicapped children and the secretaries whose personal touch has eased the pain of many a scraped knee to create a community that cares deeply about the education of its young people.

Their efforts are supplemented by a variety of private schools, funded by tuition fees, which offer their own brand of high-quality education. Especially numerous are schools following the Montessori philosophy. Although a few private schools include the elementary and high school grades or offer tutoring for slow learners, most are preschools which combine daytime care and educational services. Like in every other municipality across the province, the demand for day-care is far outstripping supply, and waiting lists are common. Indeed, intense pressure is being exerted by parents, religious groups, and social agencies to persuade governments that day-care is a public need deserving of increased funding.

The educational needs of those at the other end of the age spectrum are not ignored either. The boards of education offer continuing education courses for adults pursuing personal development or secondary-school credits in a wide range of academic and general interest subjects. Also offered are specialized subjects including English as a Second Language, Basic Literacy, English in the Workplace, Citizenship, and Driver Education.

Adult education is also provided by Seneca College of Applied Arts and Technology which, although centred in Metropolitan Toronto, has a Markham campus. A well-equipped computer centre makes computer training, at both advanced and beginner levels, available to local residents and businesses. In addition, the college offers a selection of other continuing education and career-oriented courses.

There is no university in Markham, but the main campus of York University is located not too far to the southwest. However, a group of local citizens is beginning to discuss the possibility of creating a private university in the area, to be at least partially funded by the corporate community.

The private sector offers technical and career training, too. For instance, Toronto-Buttonville International Airport provides complete recreational and professional training for pilots. Thousands of pilots have graduated from the Toronto Airways Flying School, many of whom have actively pursued careers with major airlines.

Many locally based national and multinational corporations have their own in-house training facilities. One notable example is Magna International Inc., which has a Technical Training Centre designed to help fulfill the company's need for skilled tool and die makers and other technical trades. Its modern classrooms and shop facilities have the latest in machinery and equipment. On completion of their training, students work in a Magna operating unit to complete the requirements for trade certification.

Providing a Social Safety Net

Social services allow Markham's residents to move beyond the bricks and mortar of new subdivisions to shape a community of caring. A wide variety of service agencies and volunteer organizations provides a framework of social support and acts as an effective agent for change within the town.

Many of these services are offered municipally through the York Region Health and Social Services Committee under the authority of the Medical Officer of Health, whose jurisdiction extends across York Region which includes Markham. The most visible members of this Public Health Unit are, of course, its nurses. Schoolchildren know them well, as do those confined to their homes by illness or disability, women who are pregnant, and seniors with health concerns. Also in place is a Home Care program which provides an alternative to hospital care for people of all ages. In addition, Public Health Inspectors oversee the sanitary and safety conditions that exist in both public and private buildings throughout the town.

The Markham Mobility Bus is another municipal service for those with special needs. It runs specially designed vehicles that allow physically handicapped residents to travel at their leisure throughout the town.

Many of the town's social service agencies and groups are sheltered under the umbrella of the Markham Neighbourhood

Support Centre. The Markham Family Life Centre, Family and Children's Services, Home Support Services, Big Brothers of York, Big Sisters of York, and the York Region Association for Children and Adults with Learning Disabilities are just some of the agencies sharing this innovative centre's space and administrative support services.

Another umbrella group, the United Way of York Region, also has its offices in Markham, giving it a high local profile as it collects over one million dollars annually across the region for more than 30 social service agencies. Other aspects of Markham's social support net include an emergency housing registry for youths, addiction services, credit counselling, and a food bank.

The Markham Mobility Bus transports physically handicapped residents throughout the town. Photo by Glen Jones

Keeping the Body Healthy

Health care has been an important aspect of life in Markham since the first settlers arrived in their wagons. Among the incredible hardships endured by the early pioneers were illness, injury, and disease. And in those days, there were no miracle drugs to help. But the settlers brought with them family talismans, charms, and spells, as well as a wealth of knowledge about remedies using plants.

Nearly every home had an herb garden which supplied horehound for colds, camomile for a poison antidote and for stomach ailments, and sage for cooking. The resin from the plentiful pine trees was mixed with fat and used to heal cuts and abrasions. Herbalists became an integral part of the community and one, Josephus Reesor (1820-1916), earned quite a reputation as a cancer doctor.

Less believable in these modern times of scientific theory are stories of two celebrated "charmers" who lived in the

Participation House, located in front of
the Markham/Stouffville Hospital,
provides support for profoundly
disabled adults. Photo by Jack Holman

Markham area, John Hoover and Mrs. Barkis Reesor. It is said
that people travelled great distances to receive Mrs. Reesor's
help, including a child who was suffering terribly from eczema
but was immediately cured after seeing her. In fact, there are
many tales of charms and spells being used to cure both ani-
mals and humans.

Like all rural communities, Markham depended largely on
the knowledge of the local country doctor. Using horse and
buggy, he would travel from home to home as required, admin-
istering medicines for diptheria, whooping cough, scarlet fever,
typhoid, consumption, and smallpox. Most children were born
at home with the help of a midwife. However, in 1938, a nursing
home was opened where many of the town's babies of that era
were born. Once a hospital was built in York (later to be
renamed Toronto) and the railway constructed in 1871,
Markham residents could travel there for treatment. A horse-
drawn ambulance would take them to Markham Station, where
they transferred to the train for the journey south.

In modern Markham, health care is much more accessible.

There are local chapters of more than 20 volunteer health support organizations ranging from the Arthritis Society and the Association for Autistic Children to the Canadian National Institute for the Blind, the Heart and Stroke Foundation, the Canadian Red Cross, and St. John Ambulance.

There are also dozens of clinics operated by physicians specializing in all areas of medicine from obstetrics to dentistry, from cosmetic surgery to cardiology, from pediatrics to rheumatology. There is even an exclusive private surgery facility, called Shouldice Hospital, located on a wooded ravine property on Bayview Avenue in Thornhill.

But the centrepiece of health care in Markham is the brand new Markham/Stouffville Hospital, which opened its doors in early 1990. Work on the hospital, which sits on 50 acres at the Ninth Line and Highway 7 in the town's extreme east end, began back in 1987. But the community had dreamt of a hospital of its own as far back as 1966, when 15 people from Markham and neighboring Stouffville met to discuss the feasibility of a hospital to serve their respective communities. One interested resident, Arthur Latcham, went so far as to donate the property on which the hospital would eventually be built.

The 244-bed hospital employs more than 800 people and incorporates the most up-to-date designs and operational concepts, ensuring that Markham's residents will have a first-class facility to serve their health care needs for many years into the future.

Much of the financing for the hospital came from within the community. A public fund-raising campaign was entered into heartily by citizens, old and young, who raised $5 million of the $75 million

These seniors reside in Union Villa, a residence with more than 160 units. Photo by Dawn Goss. Courtesy, First Light

cost. Money was pledged by both private and corporate citizens and raised through musical and theatrical benefits, garage sales, and a variety of other public campaigns during the half-decade prior to the hospital's opening. When the doors at last swung open to welcome staff, patients, and visitors, it was a proud monument to the unstinting, enthusiastic efforts of so many citizens and to the freely given talents of volunteers at every level of the project.

Sixty-four of the hospital's beds are used for chronic care patients, many of them elderly. But there are several other facilities for disabled and elderly people as well. For instance, a 20-

OPPOSITE: This sculpture stands on the Union Villa grounds. Photo by Dawn Goss. Courtesy, First Light

LEFT: Markham residents look to local churches to provide social and spiritual nurturing. Pictured here is Central United Church. Photo by Winston Fraser

year-old building that most Markhamites were unaware of until the hospital began to grow behind it is home to 38 profoundly disabled adults. It is called Participation House because it is truly "the house that participation built," another community effort to look after its less fortunate residents.

Markham also looks after its more mobile senior citizens. In the face of high residential real estate costs, a variety of non-profit housing and activity centres have been built in an effort to keep up with the ever-increasing need for affordable housing for seniors.

Construction of a $15-million housing and activities centre for senior adults and disabled persons is scheduled for completion in the early 1990s. Encompassing 150 one- and two-bedroom apartments, the project also features a 10,300-square-foot activities and recreational centre. The complex is located just steps from the Main Street of Markham Village, allowing easy access to shopping and other services. Spearheaded by a group called Markham Older Adults in Action, the project was fostered by the Markham Interchurch Committee for Affordable Housing (MICAH), which is supported by 12 area churches.

Also catering to seniors who want to live as independently as possible is the non-profit Unionville Home Society, which runs a 17-acre complex near Highway 7 and Main Street in Unionville. The society, initiated in 1967 by the Unionville Council of Churches, constructed Union Villa, a residence with more than 160 units featuring both self-contained apartments and individual rooms, an infirmary, a therapeutic centre, a cafeteria, and lounges.

In 1979 and 1980, 92 bungalows were added to the complex. These residences, called Heritage Village, were the first of their kind in Canada and are complemented by a two-storey recreational centre which is often used by community groups for meetings and events. Then, in 1988, the Home Society initiated another first by creating the 122-unit Wyndham Gardens complex. This apartment-type residence offers a lifetime lease/purchase plan that is unique in Canada. Residents pay a monthly maintenance fee as condominium owners do, but when they leave, they or their estate are entitled to 90 percent of the unit's resale value.

Other facilities like Markhaven, a Mennonite home for senior citizens that has grown from what was once the only non-profit nursing home in Ontario, and Glynnwood, an exclusive facility in Thornhill that bills itself as Canada's premier retirement residence, ensure diversity of housing for the town's senior citizens.

Much of the money for the construction of these facilities and financing for many ongoing projects to aid their residents comes from community service clubs. When the Markham-Unionville Lions Club celebrated its 30th Charter Anniversary in 1973, its financial contributions to the community during its history totalled more than $140,000. Funds raised by this group alone have built swimming and wading pools, contributed to the old Markham arena, helped save another arena in

Unionville, and purchased a vehicle for Participation House.

Other service clubs are equally as active and generous in their support of activities and facilities that enhance the quality of life in Markham. The Kinsmen and Kinettes clubs help organize the annual Santa Claus Parade, and many groups provide food services at outdoor festivals and other events. Service clubs also conduct seasonal drives to collect funds and food to help their less fortunate neighbors. The Canadian Progress Club, Kiwanis Club, Knights of Columbus, Optimist Club, Rotary Club, B'nai Brith Lodge, and University Women's Club all have local chapters.

Religion

With their physical needs taken care of, Markham residents look to local churches to provide social and spiritual nurturing. A variety of religious groups have traditionally been represented, from the Methodist circuit riders who zealously converted groups of rural residents at camp meetings to the Mennonites who were fully organized as early as 1808 to the German Lutherans who constructed Bethesda Church in Unionville Village in 1862, a building whose spire still punctuates the village's skyline. In fact, many of the old churches still stand, and progress has even preserved a few small cemetery plots beside which churches once stood that were the religious and social centres of now-vanished communities.

The multitude of religious denominations in modern Markham reflect the town's growing multicultural and ethnic character. Virtually every major faith is represented, and many of the churches have social outreach programs of their own. Information about them all is available through Information Markham, an aptly named community information service that handles residents' inquiries confidentially and free of charge. Its staff members are warm, friendly, and ready to provide assistance, as a neighbour would help a neighbour.

Many of the workers at Information Markham are volunteers, as are a large number of the people involved in all of the city's helping organizations. In fact, the volunteer ethic is alive and well in Markham, co-ordinated by a Volunteer Bureau which is located, along with many of the agencies its volunteers help, in the Markham Neighbourhood Support Centre.

Markham's many modern office buildings punctuate the landscape and symbolize the town's strong position as a business and high-tech centre. Photo by Dawn Goss. Courtesy, First Light

Stepping into the Future

The gold and white billboard at the side of a main road into Markham advertises a subdivision of new homes. It calls its product "The Prestige and Pride of Old Unionville." The advertising copywriters have done their job well; they have created a marketing phrase that aptly encapsulates the spirit of not just Unionville, but all of the Town of Markham.

It *is* a prestigious place to live and do business. And like the sign suggests, its resident citizens and companies take great pride in their community. The main sources of their pride are its visible heritage and the fact that it provides an increasingly rare combination of rural and urban life.

Maintaining that precious mix of rural and urban, old and new, weathered pine and shiny steel, presents an ongoing challenge. The realization that the town's traditional "four corners"—a century-old term for the town centre—has slowly shifted westward has taken residents, both old and new, by surprise. Whereas the core was once the intersection where the old village first grew, at Highway 7 and Main Street, the focus is now on the glass-and-granite intersection of highways 7 and 404.

This change has come at a time when the population is also growing—from 31,000 in 1971 to more than 135,000 in 1989 and a projected 200,000 by the year 2000—and when housing is being built at an average rate of more than 2,000 units per year.

Yes, the sleepy rural town has changed radically. The way in which the rural village of the 1930s experienced growth is noth-

Each fall the pumpkin harvest in rural Markham yields an abundance of these potential jack-o'-lanterns. Photo by Pete Ryan. Courtesy, First Light

ing compared to the challenges accompanying the heady growth of the 1980s. And Markham's small-town management style has struggled to catch up with the metamorphosis to major commercial centre. Citizens used to trust their elected government to make sensible decisions and keep taxes down, which it did from 1977 to 1985. These days, however, citizens include people living in $500,000 homes and corporations with billion-dollar budgets who demand answers to their questions.

And hard questions they are—questions about traffic jams, inadequate public transit, threats to the environment, and crowded schools. Ratepayers ask whether continued growth is desirable just for the sake of growth. They wonder whether the town's borders should be pushed any further northward to eat up more farmers' fields, many of which are already owned by speculators who are convinced they will eventually be re-zoned for industrial use. In short, residents are demanding that the superb quality of life, for which they moved to Markham in the first place, be preserved.

Fortunately for the future of the town, the spirit of enterprise that seeks to secure that very future is tempered by a pragmatic approach to problem-solving. The need to address problems and cope with growth and change is giving rise to a spirit of co-operation among the civic and provincial governments, business community, ratepayers, and social agencies. An infrastructure to support the rapid rate of growth is now being put into place.

Tony Roman, who was mayor when the growth spurt began a decade ago and had moved on to federal politics, was re-elected as mayor in 1988 on a mandate to address the citizens' concerns about their town's future. At the time of his re-election, Mayor Roman said:

It is my personal objective to see that Markham is a well-planned and efficient municipality which can effectively meet the needs of our residential and corporate citizens . . . I would like to quote Sir Frederick G. Banting who said, "It is not within the power of the properly constructed human mind to be satisfied. Progress would cease if this were the case. The greatest joy of life is to accomplish . . . I am a firm believer in the theory that you can do or be anything that you wish in this world, within reason, if you are prepared to make the sacrifices, think and work hard enough and long enough."

Modern Markhamites appear prepared, as they have been since William Berczy arrived in 1794, to think and work hard to reach their potential and to help their town continue on its path to greatness. They have realized the importance of both managing current growth and planning for its ramifications.

As the last decade of the twentieth century begins, Markham has not only stepped into the future but has its feet firmly planted there. Its excellent quality of life, steady economic growth, and strong position as a business and high-tech centre ensure for Markham a glowing, prosperous future.

II

Markham's
Enterprises

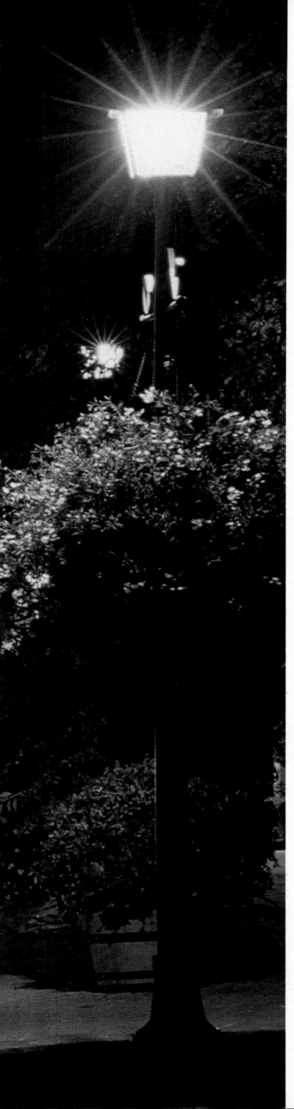

E I G H T

Networks

Markham's energy, health-

care, and transportation providers offer area residents

the best in urban services.

Photo by Dawn Goss

MARKHAM HYDRO ELECTRIC COMMISSION

The modern Markham Hydro Electric Commission facility on Warden Avenue.

As with more than 300 other municipal utilities in Ontario, Markham Hydro Electric Commission, is a publicly owned, non-profit corporation that exists to provide an essential service at the lowest-possible cost, while maintaining the highest standards of reliability and safety.

Although the utility was only established in 1979, it has grown along with the town, innovating, expanding, and developing a very progressive reputation.

Markham Hydro purchases its electricity from Ontario Hydro, which generates and sells it at cost. This purchase represents up to 80 percent of electricity costs, and, through careful budgeting and effective financial controls, Markham Hydro Electric Commission is able to keep the cost to its consumers at the lowest-possible level.

Markham Hydro's history can be traced back to 1919, when the municipal corporation of the Village of Markham signed an agreement with the Hydro Electric Power Commission of Ontario to supply electrical power in the village. The utility served the rural village well for six decades, but in 1979 a restructured Markham Hydro Electric Commission was created to deal with the faster-paced urban growth. The new utility had a staff of 24 and a customer base of approximately 25,000. Just 10 years later a staff of close to 150 serves more than 46,000 customers.

As a public utility Markham Hydro is owned by the customers it serves. Customers elect officials to oversee their utility's operation. During their three-year term commissioners set policies, supervise the retail sale of electricity rates, monitor finances, approve spending, and establish overall policy direction for staff to follow. They act as public spokespeople on all matters affecting the utility and offer an excellent system for public accountability.

In the ensuing years the commission has overseen a multitude of changes and innovations. One change that created a good deal of publicity was the use of on-site billing for reading meters and processing accounts. Markham was the first electric utility in Canada to utilize this cost-effective system, beginning in 1981, despite strong opposition from Canada Post. This computerized billing system enables the meter to be read, and a bill to be generated and delivered all in the span of a few minutes.

In 1981, to accommodate the ever-increasing growth in Markham, the utility selected a site for a much needed new headquarters building. When it opened in 1983, it was considered one of the most modern and up-to-date facilities in Canada. Both futuristic and energy efficient, the 100,000-square-foot, three-storey atrium building occupies 33 acres along with a garage, warehouse, and outdoor storage.

One of Markham Hydro's most important technological advancements was the installation of its Supervisory Control and Data Acquisition (SCADA) system. This state-of-the-art system provides constant monitoring, assessment, and operation of the utility's entire distribution system

An example of the modern vehicle fleet at Markham Hydro.

through the use of microcomputer two-way communications and enables operators to restore power more quickly to areas affected by power interruptions.

Two other major capital expenditures were made in the late 1980s by Markham Hydro to cope with the explosive growth of the town. Two transformer stations were commissioned, and another is planned to provide reliability to the system and meet the growing load demand of existing and future customers.

Among Markham Hydro's many innovations was the implementation in 1984 of equal billing through pre-authorized payment. Markham Hydro was one of the country's first utilities to implement this cost-effective convenient method of payment. A pioneering PCB decontamination program was introduced in 1988. And, more recently, an experimental project was announced whereby electricity could be generated by utilizing the differential in natural gas pressure when it is reduced by the wholesaler for residential distribution.

In addition to supplying electrical power to both residential and business customers, Markham Hydro

has a strong commitment to its customers and has adopted an active marketing plan that promotes energy management, safety and product knowledge through community presentations, awards, literature, and newsletters.

Markham Hydro has successfully responded to the challenge of facilitating the tremendous construction boom. High-density development in Markham has clearly shown the co-operation between utili-

Customer-oriented staff are always ready to assist customers with their inquiries.

ties, developers, and municipalities.

Its progressive management style and innovative marketing programs earned Markham Hydro the title Utility of the Year in 1986. And, for its excellent in-house safety program and safe work practices, it was awarded the Low Accident Frequency Award by the Electrical Utilities Safety Association of Ontario in both 1987 and 1988.

Because of the tremendous growth of the town, Markham Hydro Electric Commission has been faced with numerous challenges. Consequently, the search for new technologies and improved operating methods that has made it an award-winning and progressive utility will continue to be an ongoing process for many years to come. As its mandate declares, "Markham Hydro Electric Commission is the servant of the people, and one of its sole objectives is to provide its residential, commercial, and industrial customers with the most efficient and economical electrical service."

The state-of-the-art control room at Markham Hydro Electric Commission.

SHOULDICE HOSPITAL

What began as the vision of one man became a reality that has, since its inception, alleviated suffering for close to 200,000 people, including some internationally known personalities and dignitaries from all parts of the world.

Dr. Earle Shouldice, the founder of the Shouldice Hospital in Thornhill, created a unique facility that has become one of the largest private hospitals in Ontario. Located on a 23-acre estate, Shouldice Hospital is a single-specialty facility, performing only abdominal hernia repairs.

The hospital was opened in 1945 to serve more than 200 civilians seeking Dr. Shouldice's abdominal hernia operation. This special operation initially was developed to allow recruits suffering from hernias to enter the Army. A six-room nursing home was purchased in Toronto and converted to a private hospital, and later in 1953 a country estate on Bayview Avenue was converted into the hospital, which is to-

day jokingly referred to by patients as the "Shouldice Hilton."

Entrance to the 74,000-square-foot hospital is through the front door of the original private residence, which has been retained to create a friendly, home-like atmosphere. This part of the hospital houses administration, reception, and offices; a new wing, completed in 1969, houses the rest of the hospital—a modern, state-of-the-art facility.

The hospital is designed around Dr. Shouldice's unique treatment philosophy, which includes early ambulation, light physical exercise, and the positive effect of patient socialization. Wide, carpeted corridors, tastefully decorated lounges, a central dining room, and a nine-hole putting green encourage patients to move around the hospital. Semi-private rooms, with a total of 89 licensed beds, all have a view of the property's extensive gardens.

The actual surgical procedure is also innovative, and most operations

are under local anaesthetic. Dr. Shouldice received worldwide recognition for it and a variety of other medical advances. In spite of the fact that 13 full-time surgeons perform an average of 30 operations daily and the average stay is just four days, there is a regular waiting list of more than 1,000 patients. One-quarter of the patients travel to Thornhill from the United States. Others are attracted by word of mouth from all parts of Canada and Europe.

Respect, compassion, and competence are the tenets by which Shouldice Hospital operates. It goes out of its way to make all patients feel at home, no matter how far away from home they might be. This might be the only hospital in the world where patients are actually eager to return for a reunion.

Shouldice Hospital is a single-surgery facility specializing in abdominal hernia repairs. Pictured here is the hospital, located on 30 acres in Markham.

GLYNNWOOD RETIREMENT RESIDENCE

The logo of Glynnwood Retirement Residence depicts a Canadian goose landing in front of the sun just slightly below the horizon. After a long flight, the bird has chosen to land, yet is able to continue on its journey when it pleases. The residents of Glynnwood have chosen to live there, not as a place to spend just a few years, but as a place to continue living and enjoying life without restrictions.

The residence was founded in 1981 on the grounds of the Shouldice Hospital by Dr. Byrnes Shouldice and his sister, Mrs. William Urquhart. The need for a finely appointed, yet competitively priced residence for seniors had been made clear to them by the loneliness of their father after the death of their mother. So they developed what has become the optimum solution for mentally alert, physically healthy, and active seniors who wish to maintain an independent lifestyle without the cares of a house or apartment.

The award-winning, six-storey building, which sits on 6.5 acres of cultivated gardens and natural woods, has 180 suites, mostly studios and one bedrooms. All have tinted glass, balconies, four-piece baths, and kitchenettes. A few larger suites are also available. Since the principal idea of Glynnwood is for residents to have their own homes, suites come unfurnished so that residents can decorate them with their own favorite belongings.

Life at Glynnwood is like that in a first-class residential hotel.

Approximately 100 caring staff members help residents maintain a high standard of living. This includes maid service and emergency nursing supervision. A wonderfully appointed dining room serves breakfast, lunch, and dinner with a varied menu selection and frequent special-event dinners that give the chef a chance to show off his talents. A dining room can be reserved for private functions. A hairdresser comes to the in-house beauty salon three days per week, a banking service visits once per week, a dry cleaner picks up and delivers, and there are laundry facilities on each floor.

As in a resort hotel, the 24-hour reception desk is the hub of Glynnwood's active community life. Residents enjoy movie nights, pub nights, afternoon teas, card and games rooms, billiards, bridge, shuffleboard, a putting green, and an organized physical fitness program. There is even an area for individual vegetable or flower gardens. Intellectual and cultural pursuits are also popular, ranging from lecture series, movies, and live entertainment, to a well-stocked library and van trips to theatre festivals in Stratford and Niagara-on-the-Lake.

To live at Glynnwood Retirement Residence is to live in a very special place—a combination of comfort and security, of beauty and grace, of community activity and privacy.

The exterior of Glynnwood Retirement Residence.

TORONTO AIRWAYS LTD.

Airports have a significant impact on communities. One airport, strategically located at Highway 404 just north of Highway 7 in Markham, has had a huge effect on the vibrant economy of Markham and the Metro Toronto area.

Toronto-Buttonville Airport, privately owned and operated by Toronto Airways Ltd., has been called Canada's finest general aviation airport. It is also one of the nation's busiest—the eighth busiest in 1987. Featuring an instrument approach and fully equipped terminal facilities, it handles a variety of air services, including executive business charters, pleasure flights, commuter flights, and private business planes.

From a meager grass strip in 1940, the airport has been developed to accommodate an ever-growing demand. It was purchased by Toronto Airways in 1959, and the control tower and runways were built in the intervening years. All the development has been privately financed without public funds, subsidies, or grants from any level of government.

The statistics are impressive.

The 180-acre facility is home to 340 aircraft and employs more than 300 people. More than 190,000 takeoffs and landings took place there in 1988. Since 1967, 4.5 million landings and takeoffs have occurred there. About 90,000 customers are served by the airport in an average year. More than 100 companies have planes based there, and another 80 use the charter service. As of September 4, 1989, Canadian Partner is operating a high-frequency Dash 8 commuter service between Toronto-Buttonville and Ottawa and Dorval.

In spite of the amount of traffic, the airport is one of Canada's best kept secrets. One of the reasons for that is a management philosophy of operating the airport in harmony with the surrounding community. Although the community has never asked for noise restrictions, a policy is maintained to request noisy aircraft to not use the facility. And to further the image of a good community corporate citizen, Toronto Airways participates in the Markham community by sponsoring various local charitable causes.

The Buttonville Airport.

The airport is a small community in itself, with close to 20 businesses and organizations located on the site. These include companies that sell and service aircraft, two air ambulance services, and Transport Canada's Toronto Air Radio, which provides weather and flight-planning services. There is even a small radio studio on site for traffic reporters for two Toronto radio stations who fly from Buttonville. Canada Customs also maintains a five-days-per-week service for the convenience of flying businesspeople.

Toronto Airways Flying School, together with Seneca College's aviation technology course, provides complete flight training—from the private pilot's course to advanced training for professional pilots. To round out the full spectrum of aviation services, there is an on-site Ministry of Transportation Flight Examination Centre, as well as the first aviation medical office to be located at an airport.

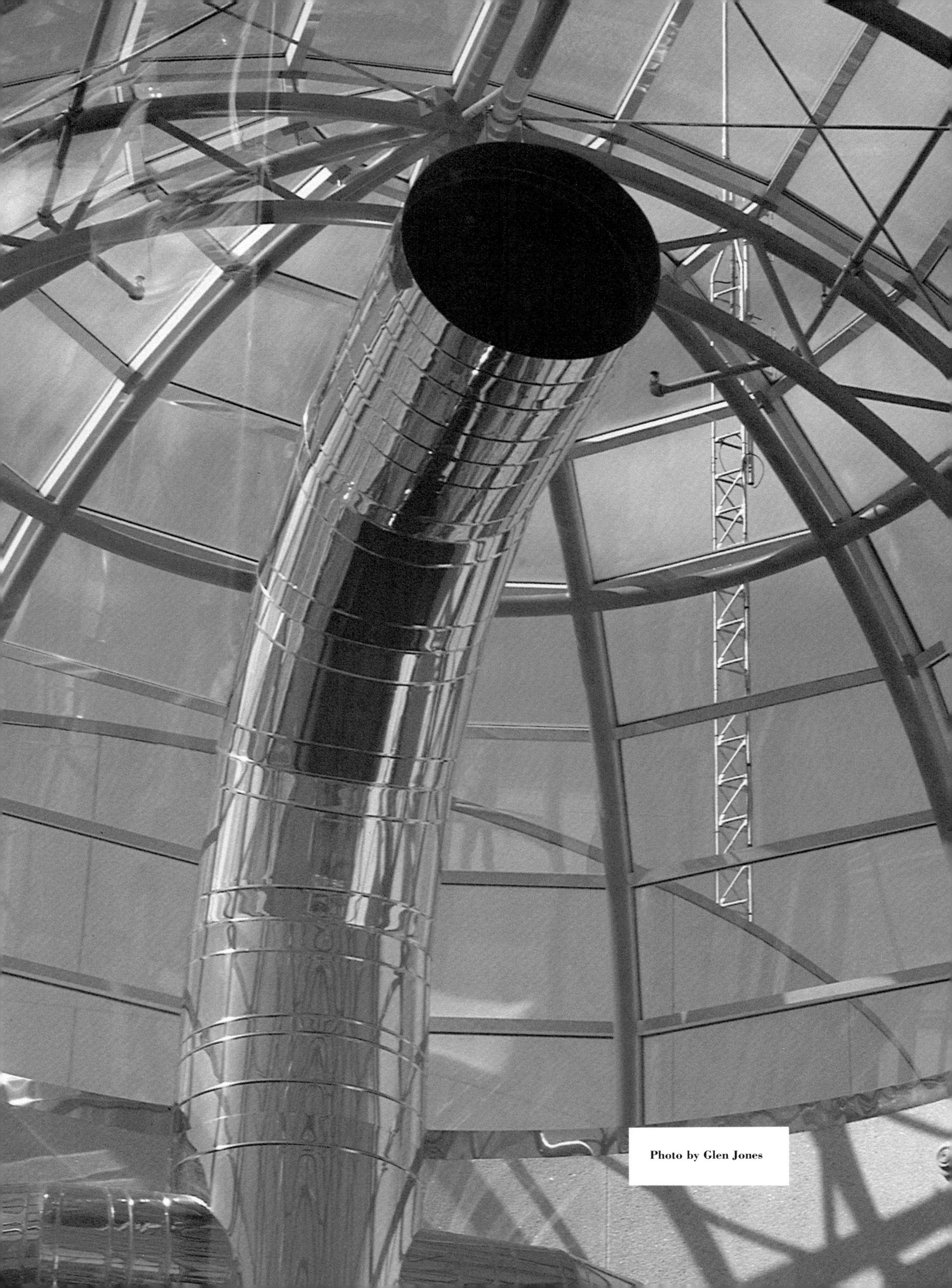

Photo by Glen Jones

Industry

Producing and distributing goods for individuals and businesses, Markham area industry provides employment for many of its residents.

Photo by Pete Ryan

LEVI STRAUSS & CO. (CANADA) INC.

The corporate roots of Levi Strauss & Co. (Canada) Inc. date back to the California Gold Rush of the 1850s. Since then, the Levi's® name has become synonymous with denim blue jeans worldwide. A look at the history of the company, whose Canadian headquarters is in Markham, is, in essence, a look at the birth and evolution of blue jeans.

When 24-year-old Levi Strauss arrived in San Francisco from New York in 1853, it was with the intention of opening a dry goods business. But by the time he reached his destination, he had sold most of his merchandise to passengers aboard the ship he was travelling on. What remained of his supplies was mainly canvas for tents and wagon covers. Upon learning that miners and prospectors needed durable and well-made pants, Strauss took his heavy canvas to a tailor,

and the world's first pair of jeans was born. As word spread quickly of the quality of Levi's pants, he produced dozens more pairs and soon exhausted his original supply of material.

At this point he switched to a sturdy fabric made in Nimes, France, called "serge de Nimes." Later, the name of the fabric was conveniently shortened to "denim." With the development of an indigo dye, its brown color gave way to the now-familiar deep blue. Rivets were eventually used to strengthen the pockets of the pants, as miners had complained that the weight of gold nuggets caused their pockets to rip.

It wasn't until the mid-1930s that the famous Red Tab was added to the right-hand hip pocket and the company began referring to the pants as "jeans." The term was derived from the cotton trousers (called "genes" by the French) worn

Although a wholly owned subsidiary of the San Francisco-based parent company, Levi Strauss & Co. (Canada) Inc. functions with virtual autonomy and is responsible for its own raw material suppliers, manufacturing, distribution, sales, and advertising.

by sailors from Genoa, Italy.

As Levi's® jeans grew in popularity, so did the fortunes of Levi Strauss & Co. At present the firm's various apparel products are sold in more than 70 countries, making it one of the world's largest clothing manufacturers. More than 32,000 employees work in the company's factories, offices, and warehouses throughout some 30 countries.

In the early 1960s Levi Strauss & Co. acquired majority interest in one of its major rivals, the Canadian-founded Great Western Garment Company (GWG). A decade later it purchased the remainder of GWG, and the two firms have operated as a single corporate entity since 1981. Fittingly, the two organizations share not only a long tradition of manufacturing quality garments, but also a deep-rooted belief in displaying a strong sense of responsibility toward their employees and the community.

At Levi Strauss & Co., the philosophy of social responsibility began with the firm's founder, who devoted considerable time and resources to many charities and organizations. To perpetuate Strauss' humanitarian ideals, the company formed community affairs departments and community involvement teams in the 1970s. Operating from corporate facilities worldwide, the teams are made up of volunteer employees who help identify social issues and worthwhile causes within their respective communities. The company, in turn, provides financial support to the charitable projects and organizations with which the employees are involved.

Another belief of Levi Strauss & Co. is that it should contribute to the economic infrastructure of a country in which it sells its products. In Canada, for example, all GWG garments and more than 95 percent of Levi's® products are manufactured domestically.

In order to preserve the firm's independence and family values, full ownership of Levi Strauss & Co. was restored to the descendants of Strauss in 1985.

While a wholly owned subsidiary of its San Francisco-based parent company, Levi Strauss & Co. (Canada) Inc. functions with virtual autonomy and is responsible for its own raw material suppliers, manufacturing, distribution, sales, and advertising. It has sewing plants in Stoney Creek and Cornwall, Ontario, and in Edmonton; a finishing plant for washing and labeling in Brantford, Ontario; a distribution centre in Toronto; and sales offices in Toronto, Montreal, and Calgary.

Formed in 1972, the operation was originally based in Toronto's Don Mills until 1988, when it relocated its head office to a modern 57,000-square-foot facility in Markham. More than 200 staff work from the location and are responsible for areas that include design, marketing, sales, and administration.

As part of its corporate philosophy, Levi Strauss & Co. (Canada) Inc. believes its strength lies in its people. Therefore it strives to eliminate bureaucracy and over-management, creating an environment where individuals can reach their potential without needless constraints. Management's main role is to offer employees a strong sense of direction and corporate values while encouraging them to act with initiative and independence.

Over the years Levi Strauss & Co. products have been associated with the highest standards of quality—a direct result of the convictions of the company's founder. This tradition plays an integral role in the present-day success of Levi Strauss & Co. (Canada) Inc. and makes it a corporate citizen that Markham can point to with pride.

Levi Strauss & Co. (Canada) Inc. moved its corporate headquarters to a modern 57,000-square-foot facility in Markham. More than 200 staff work from the location and are responsible for areas that include design, marketing, sales, and administration.

CYANAMID CANADA INC.

A recent arrival to Markham's corporate environment, Cyanamid Canada Inc. is, nonetheless, a firm with long-established Canadian roots.

Founded as an American company in 1907, Cyanamid opened its first plant that same year in Niagara Falls, Ontario, using the abundant hydro-electric power generated by the falls in the production of calcium cyanamide—the world's first synthetic fertilizer. Expansion proved to be rapid as other agricultural products were added to the Cyanamid line. In 1934 Cyanamid Canada was spun from its parent firm, American Cyanamid Company.

Today the Cyanamid organization boasts a number of pioneering firsts in the research and development of biotechnology and chemical products for medical, agricultural, industrial, and consumer markets.

Cyanamid Canada moved its head office to Markham from nearby Willowdale in 1987. The facility employs a staff of 250, which oversees Cyanamid Canada's various domestic operations and the import and marketing of many other of the organization's more than 3,000 products. Globally the firm sells its products in some 135 countries and employs more than 34,000 people.

The Medical Products Group comprises the Lederle Laboratories Division and the Medical Services Division. Lederle is a leader in the research and manufacture of ethical pharmaceuticals for cancer, cardiovascular, and dermatological diseases as well as in the development of nutritional supplements for the consumer health market. The Medical Devices Division includes Davis & Geck, a manufacturer of surgical devices; Accufex Microsurgical Inc., a leading supplier of arthroscopic surgical devices; and Storz Instrument Company, a major producer of ophthalmic surgical instruments.

The Crop Protection Division manufactures and markets a wide range of insecticides, herbicides, and fungicides used by farmers to dramatically increase crop quality and yield. The Animal Products Division produces vaccines and feed additives for both livestock and broad-based veterinary practice.

The Chemical Products Division is a leading supplier of chemicals with applications in the aerospace, automotive, electronic, food and drug, mining, pulp and paper, steel manufacturing, and water- and waste-management industries. The

Cyanamid Canada employs a staff of 250 that oversees the firm's various domestic operations and the import and marketing of many other of the organization's more than 3,000 products.

Carbide Products Division produces and markets calcium carbide—a versatile chemical that is used to produce a broad range of consumer and industrial chemicals.

Cyanamid Canada's affiliated company, Shulton Canada Inc., is a leading manufacturer of personal care products. These include well-known brand names such as Old Spice (toiletries), Breck (hair care products), and Pine-Sol (liquid cleaner).

An innovator in many high-technology areas, Cyanamid Canada Inc. is a fine example of the type of leading-edge companies that have chosen to call Markham home.

In 1987 Cyanamid Canada Inc. moved its head office to Markham.

FORD ELECTRONICS MANUFACTURING CORPORATION

A view of the office and plant of Ford Electronics that was built in 1984 and currently contains 290,000 square feet of space.

As Canada's largest exporter of automotive electronics, Markham's Ford Electronics Manufacturing Corporation has played a key role in the technological advancement of automobiles built by its parent firm, the Ford Motor Company.

Electronic technology has enabled automotive engines to start on the coldest of mornings. It has vastly improved fuel economy and handling performance in comparison to vehicles of the 1960s and 1970s. It has resulted in less automotive maintenance through continuous improvement in electronic component reliability and the replacement of complex mechanical functions with electronics. And it has provided vehicles with conveniences such as home-quality stereo sound and climate-control systems.

The main components manufactured at Ford Electronics' Markham plant are automotive audio systems, electronic instrument clusters, automatic temperature controls, warning light systems, and airbag and seat belt controls. A 64,000-square-foot plant expansion was completed in 1989 to meet increased product demand and to manufacture two new product lines—vehicle anti-theft modules and programmable speedometer/odometer modules.

Utilizing a variety of manual and automated manufacturing processes, Ford Electronics' Markham operation has a total of 1,500 employees and 290,000 square feet of floor space. The facility relies on high-technology equipment such as automatic-guided vehicles that transport parts, computer-integrated manufacturing systems that monitor quality and performance levels, and automatic vision-testing equipment that scans products for defects.

In 1989 the plant became the first Ford Electronics plant to receive the Ford Motor Company's prestigious Preferred Quality Q1 Award, for achieving outstanding quality levels in its products. To earn the award, the plant underwent a rigorous, yearlong test in which its products were rated by Ford quality standards and customer plants worldwide.

In order to achieve high standards of product quality and continually improve manufacturing methods, Ford Electronics places a strong emphasis on employee teamwork, involvement, and training. Another philosophy is that customer satisfaction is the guiding principle behind everything the company does.

Ford Electronics' corporate roots trace back to the U.S.-based Philco Corporation, which established Canadian operations in the early 1930s, assembling home radios at its Toronto plant. As product lines grew to include other consumer products, the firm moved to nearby Don Mills in 1954. Seven years later Philco Corporation was acquired by the Ford Motor Company and became known as the Philco-Ford Corporation. The firm discontinued production of consumer products in the mid-1970s and assumed its present name in 1984.

Serving a key function within the Ford Motor Company's Electrical and Electronics Division, Ford Electronics Manufacturing Corporation has also played a significant role in enabling Markham to become a major Canadian centre for high-technology businesses.

This automatic computer-controlled machine places electronic devices on printed wire circuit boards, which are used in the manufacture of electronic automotive parts.

CHESEBROUGH-POND'S (CANADA) INC.

When Chesebrough-Pond's selected its Markham Village site in the early 1950s, it led the way for future industrial growth in Markham.

In 1957, when the firm opened the doors of its new 56,000-square-foot manufacturing and office facility on Bullock Drive, the 11-acre parcel of land was surrounded by farms and fields. Bullock Drive, now a major thoroughfare, was then a dirt road that dead-ended at the Chesebrough site. Even then the company was a major employer, with 95 workers in a village of 3,500 people.

But Chesebrough-Pond's history begins long before the move to Markham. In addition to being a pioneering story, it is one of both innovation and corporate mergers. The latest chapter, which began in 1986, saw the company purchased by Unilever, the world's largest producer of consumer goods.

The history of the Chesebrough company dates back to the American oil boom of the mid-nineteenth century, when the first gushers were found in Pennsylvania. Robert Chesebrough had just gone into business as a manufacturer of illuminating oil. In 1959 he began experimenting with a petroleum residue known

Chesebrough-Pond's 56,000-square-foot manufacturing and office facility on Bullock Drive in Markham was opened in 1957.

as rod wax because it formed on the steel rods of oil pumps. Workmen in the field claimed the substance had miraculous healing powers. Chesebrough developed a similar wax—a semisolid that he named petroleum jelly. By the mid-1870s his firm was incorporated as the Chesebrough Manufacturing Company and was marketing the jelly under the trade name of Vaseline.

In 1881 the firm was absorbed by the Standard Oil Company and stayed under its jurisdiction for 30 years until a judicial decision ordered Standard Oil to divest itself of 33 subsidiary companies, including Chesebrough.

The first Canadian plant was built in Montreal in 1910, and expansion continued. Additional products such as Vaseline hair tonic and shampoo were added to the line. With the advent of World War II, Chesebrough developed Vaseline sterile petrolatum gauze at the request of the U.S. Army.

While Chesebrough Company was developing in the second half of the nineteenth century, so was another organization led by Theron P. Pond of Utica, New York. He had developed a remedy distilled from the witch hazel shrub that he called Pond's Extract. That product became a famous household remedy for more than 60 years and was the basis for many beauty products, including Pond's Vanishing Cream and Pond's Cold Cream. The creams entered the Canadian market in 1918, and the Pond's Extract Company of Canada Limited was formed in 1927.

In 1955 the Chesebrough Manufacturing Company and the Pond's Extract Company merged to become Chesebrough-Pond's Inc. In Canada, it became Chesebrough-Pond's (Canada) Ltd., and the Montreal Chesebrough operation was transferred to the Pond's plant in Toronto.

Shortly after came the move to Markham. Since that time additional expansion and acquisitions have taken place. The most recent chapter in the firm's history began in 1986 with its purchase by Unilever, an Anglo-Dutch business formed in

1930 with headquarters in London and Rotterdam. In Canada, Unilever markets household products such as Sunlight, Wisk, and All; Dove and Lifebuoy soaps; and food products, including Shopsy's, Imperial margarines, A&W root beer, Lipton soups, Red Rose, and Lawry's. Many other products are now manufactured, distributed, and sold nationally under the Chesebrough-Pond's corporate umbrella. These include AIM, Pepsodent, and Close-up toothpastes; Impulse Body Spray Deodorant; Lypsyl; Pears Shampoo and Con-

These household products are just a few of the many manufactured by Chesebrough-Pond's.

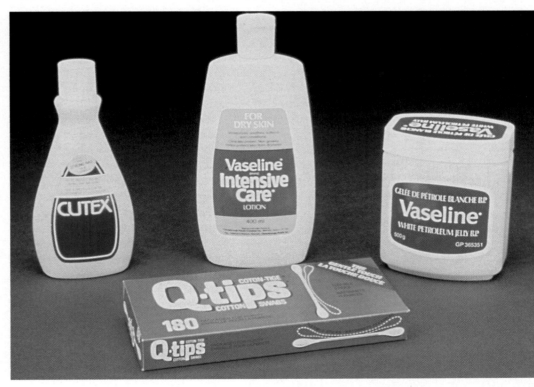

ditioner; Vaseline Intensive Care Lotions; Cutex cosmetics; Q-Tips; as well as Timotei Shampoo and Conditioner.

Since the acquisition by Unilever, new emphasis and priority have been directed to marketing. Whereas in the past relatively few new products were introduced by Chesebrough-Pond's, at least 10 were launched during a recent year.

A long-term research, development, and marketing program has been put in place to aggressively develop and launch new product lines.

Chesebrough-Pond's and Unilever both employ a progressive management style. A list of 16 corporate values refers to such desirables as an open, co-operative management style and clear opportunities for employee career develop-

ment. Also part of the code of values is the firm's intention to encourage and expect a high level of loyalty, commitment, and involvement from all its employees.

Not only are the employees involved with the company, they—and the company—are involved with the community. They have raised money for Participation House, a residence for disabled adults, and the Markham/Stouffville Hospital. Each year a sizable contribution is made to the United Way campaign, as well as other organizations. In addition, the firm sponsors teams in the Markham Youth Soccer Association, the Markham Baseball Association, and the Markham Minor Hockey Association.

The combined growth and co-operation of Chesebrough-Pond's (Canada) Inc. and Markham over the years is an excellent example of community and business growing together to mutual advantage.

RAYWAL LIMITED

Raywal Limited is both a pioneer in its field and a pioneer in Markham. As one of the early industrial residents in the John Street/Bayview Avenue area of Thornhill, it has contributed greatly to the town's economic development. In addition, it has also been a leader in the kitchen-cabinet industry in Canada.

The company dates to May 1954, when it entered business as Norden Building Products Ltd. Its function at that time was to sell windows purchased from other manufacturers. In order to better service the market, the owners decided to set up their own window-manufacturing facility. They also realized there was a bright future in kitchen-cabinet and prefabricated stair manufacturing, which until then had been constructed on the job sites. The first 6,000-square-foot factory was devoted to the manufacture of these products.

Raywal thus became one of the first Canadian companies to offer prefabricated kitchen cabinets and bathroom vanities. Until the advent of prefabricated cabinets, amenities that are now taken for granted, such as bathroom vanities, were seldom seen in any home. The launch

of prefabricated lines was appropriately timed and executed by Raywal to coincide with the increasing demand for such innovation in the building industry. Over the years, as prefabricated kitchens gained acceptance from builders, so did the number of new cabinet manufacturers; many of these have been founded by former Raywal employees. Raywal therefore established itself as a leader in this young industry.

In addition to being innovative, Raywal quickly gained a reputation for quality and reliability. After only three years in business, the rapid growth of the firm necessitated a move to a new 18,000-square-foot factory in North York. Almost immediately after the move to the new facility, the company was in need of even more space and leased additional premises nearby.

Two years later Raywal, to better accommodate and increase the manufacture of cabinets, built a 21,000-square-foot factory on Green Lane in the east end of Thornhill—an area that was later to become part of the town of Markham.

In 1963 an additional 14,000 square feet of plant and 4,000 square feet of office space were built to consolidate all its operations at the present Green Lane location. By the mid-1960s the success of the cabinet operations led to the decision to specialize solely on these products.

Today, after further expansion, the office and plant facilities cover more than 100,000 square feet and employ in excess of 200 people.

Raywal Limited remains committed to its long history of producing, installing, servicing, and guaranteeing fine kitchens not only for the many elegant new homes in Markham, but throughout Ontario.

nished, while other finishes and prefinished materials were tried to constantly improve the overall appearance and quality of the products.

Raywal has been able to maintain a high standard of craftsmanship in part due to its ability to maintain a stable and long-term skilled work force. The company is so proud and confident of its quality that it offers a two-year warranty against defects in material and workmanship. It is this continuing commitment to quality and service that Raywal's customers have come to rely on.

Throughout the years there has been a constant evolving of ideas that continues today. Various designs and types of material have been used to satisfy changing tastes and styles. The first cabinets were very primitive compared to present-day standards. Though the cabinets were custom assembled in a factory and then installed into houses, the early versions consisted of cabinets with sliding doors as opposed to today's norm of hinged doors, and materials used were of paint-grade quality. Once installed, these cabinets still had to be finished (painted) by the builder. Counter top laminate selections were also very limited. There were maybe a half-dozen colors available then as compared to the literally hundreds of colors, textures, and finishes available today.

From completely unfinished products, Raywal started introducing various degrees of finishing. Doors and drawer fronts were the first to be factory finished. It was not until 1957 that styling had progressed to the point of incorporating hinged doors into the products. In 1958 Raywal introduced its first stain-grade cabinets, and the predominant wood specie, during this stage, was ribbon-

striped mahogany. Again as with the paint-grade materials, it was only the doors and drawer fronts that were factory finished. The frames, sides, and the interiors were still essentially unfinished lumber. Other improvements such as replacing bank of drawers units with drawers above the base cabinet doors were also made at this time.

By 1960 Raywal had progressed to the stage of completely prefinishing all exposed surfaces of its cabinets. Factory-finished products offered the advantage of much higher quality finish as opposed to what could be achieved on the job sites while at the same time reducing costs to the builder. During the 1960s finishing of the interiors received special attention. In 1960 the wooden interiors were only var-

Today a wide variety of cabinetry designs are available in a full range of modular units and accessories in either frame or frameless construction. European-inspired frameless construction with concealed hinges and laminated surfaces create clean lines for the modern look. On the other hand frame construction using solid oak frames suits the more traditionally minded customer.

Raywal Limited remains committed to its long history of producing, installing, servicing, and guaranteeing fine kitchens not only for the many elegant new homes in Markham, but throughout Ontario. For more than three decades its hallmark has been service, integrity, and quality—all very fine qualities for a pioneer.

BURNDY CANADA ELECTRONICS DIVISION

The advantages of locating a business in Markham may seem obvious today. Taxes are relatively lower than surrounding municipalities, land costs are reasonable, the municipal government is supportive, and access is ideal. However, there was a time when those advantages were obvious only to those willing to look open-mindedly into the future.

As an early participant in Markham's corporate explosion, Burndy Canada's Electronics Division has shown itself to be one of those pioneers. But the company, which designs and manufactures electronic connectors, is poised for significant growth substantially greater than that of its market because of a number of other innovations.

Burndy traces its roots back to 1924, when it was formed by American utility engineer Bern Dibner to produce a special electrical connector he had designed. Burndy Canada, one of a number of international subsidiaries of Burndy Corporation, came into being in 1949 when a manufacturing facility was opened in Toronto. The Electronics Division was launched in Markham in 1974. It occupied a leased unit in one of the town's first industrial parks, on Bullock Drive. As it

grew, it gradually took over more units until it leased all 11 units in the building.

The division's growth was fuelled by its unique position in the industry in Canada. Unlike its competitors, who merely assemble their product in Canada, Burndy does all its engineering, manufacturing, and sales and marketing in Canada. Because much of its work involves developing new connectors or customizing existing designs, manufacturing in Canada gives it a distinctive edge. It enables Burndy to be flexible and responsive to customers' needs and shorten lead time between problem recognition and finished product. When necessary, the complete process has been accomplished in less than eight weeks.

Because of this service and flexibility, the firm has developed an impressive customer base of the major Canadian computer, telecommunications, and office-equipment companies, many of whom are located in Markham. Increasing emphasis is being put on this domestic market, although product is exported worldwide.

In 1989, to further its competitive advantage, Burndy moved its 100 employees into a new 60,000-

Burndy Canada Electronics Division headquarters building is located on 5.2 acres overlooking Buttonville Airport. The $6-million plant is a self-contained, world-class facility worthy of the firm's world-class engineers.

square-foot facility on 5.2 acres overlooking Buttonville Airport. The $6-million plant is a self-contained, world-class facility worthy of the firm's world-class engineers. Burndy prides itself on its complete design capability, and the new building is equipped with state-of-the-art computer-aided design (CAD) and quality-assurance laboratory equipment.

On the manufacturing end, the facility has created a whole new league for connector manufacturers in Canada. It has allowed significant production economies through increased work-flow streamlining and increased capacity through new automated production equipment purchases. The production process involves a number of diverse activities; molding, stamping, and assembling are the key ones. Much of the equipment for these processes has been custom designed and built by Burndy itself.

The facility's design is in itself innovative. It was designed by the Toronto architectural firm of Cravit Ortved and constructed by Cooper Corporation under intense consultation with Burndy executives. What resulted was an open, functional manufacturing facility that provides a clean working environment and allows for flexibility of layout. Because in the electronic connector business product life is typically short and much of the firm's business is custom work, the design allows equipment to be easily moved around as new products are introduced. All equipment and people needed to manufacture a particular product can be grouped together and regrouped to cut cycle time, materials handling, work-in-process inventory, and paperwork.

In this unique industrial complex, administrative and manufacturing functions are separated only by a glass-walled atrium walkway. This open design allows the building to function as a marketing tool: Visitors and customers can easily view the manufacturing operation from the walkway or office area. The plant's clean, efficient look inspires confidence in prospective customers.

The open feeling extends to the office environment and typifies the firm's accessible management philosophy, with even the closed-in executive offices having glass fronts. An added psychological advantage of the glass-lined walkway between plant and office is that it provides integration of the people who work in the plant with those who work in the office. Burndy management believes that having engineers aware of the manufacturing process while they are working retains the critical mind set that ensures what is designed can actually be made—and at a world-competitive price.

This practical attitude is crucial to Burndy Canada Electronics Division's aim of customer satisfaction. It is part of a worldwide corporate program built around taking a customer-focused viewpoint and also involves a system of regular internal audits and independent evaluations. The phrase "Customer Satisfaction Comes First," printed boldly on the flag flying in front of building, is more than just an empty platitude. It is part of a profile that, along with the sense of innovation that brought it to Markham in the first place, makes the company poised for a full and profitable future.

This interior view of Burndy's offices and manufacturing facilities shows the walkway separating the two divisions as well as one of the company's product displays (lower right).

MITSUBISHI ELECTRIC SALES CANADA INC.

The headquarters building of Mitsubishi Electric Sales Canada Inc. in Markham.

Mitsubishi Electric Sales Canada Inc. was created from a setback that was turned into a golden opportunity by its parent company, Mitsubishi Electric Corporation of Japan. As a result, Markham gained a corporate resident that is a world leader in the consumer electronics field, with 1989 sales surpassing $200 million.

Canadians were first introduced to Mitsubishi home entertainment products during the mid-1970s by Superior Electronics, a Montreal-based electronic products distributor. When the company ceased operations in 1979, Mitsubishi Electric Corporation decided to establish its own Canadian subsidiary to con-

tinue national marketing of the firm's home and car audio products, as well as to honor warranties on products that had already been sold in Canada. That same year Markham was selected as the site of Mitsubishi's Canadian subsidiary for two reasons: the high-technology nature of many existing companies in the area and favorable local tax rates.

By 1981 the Canadian Foreign Investment Review Agency granted Mitsubishi the right to sell Japanese-made videocassette recorders and large-screen projection televisions in Canada but insisted that the company domestically manufacture color televisions for Canadian sale. Consequently Mitsubishi entered a contract manufacturing agreement in 1982 with Electrohome Ltd. of Kitchener, Ontario, that saw Electro-

Mitsubishi Electric Sales Canada Inc., Waterloo—television factory, warehouse, and offices of the Melkit Marketing Division.

home produce Mitsubishi color television sets with Mitsubishi components. Later that year, coincidentally, Electrohome decided to vacate the consumer products market.

Mitsubishi Electric entered into an agreement with Electrohome Ltd. to use the name "Electrohome" and to hire the people in Electrohome's consumer electronics group. In January 1983 the newly formed Melkit Marketing Division (Mitsubishi Electric Kitchener) continued to sell "Electrohome"-brand product television sets produced under contract by Electrohome Ltd.

The success of the twin-brand concept eventually led to the opening of a new television manufacturing facility in nearby Waterloo, Ontario, in January 1986, where all Mitsubishi and Electrohome television sets are now made.

In addition to obtaining a new operating division, Mitsubishi's Canadian subsidiary received a new corporate name in 1983—Mitsubishi Electric Sales Canada Inc. Up to that time the firm had been known as Melco Sales Canada Inc. (Melco is an acronym for Mitsubishi Electric Corp.)

Mitsubishi Electric's faith in the Canadian electronics industry was again demonstrated in 1983, when it purchased and reopened the defunct RCA television picture-tube plant in Midland, Ontario. Under the name of Mitsubishi Electronics Industries Canada Inc., the plant rehired several hundred local employees and presently manufactures picture tubes for both Mitsubishi and Electrohome televisions, as well as for sale to domestic and export markets.

From sales of $2.2 million in its first year, Mitsubishi Canada had reached revenue of almost $100 million in 1984. To accommodate its rapidly growing business, the firm moved into its present head office facility on Woodbine Avenue that same year. It also formed its Industrial Electronics Division, which markets an ever-increasing line of electronic products, including cellular phones, facsimile machines, security and surveillance systems, computers, and a broad range of color monitors for the computer and electronic information-transmission fields.

Mitsubishi Canada's 51,000-square-foot Markham head office is mainly involved in sales, marketing, and warehousing functions for the consumer electronics and industrial electronics divisions. Similar functions for the Electrohome line are conducted by the Melkit Marketing Division in Waterloo.

The television picture tube factory in Midland, Ontario, Mitsubishi Electronics Industries Canada Inc.

The firm's corporate service division, which moved to nearby Richmond Hill from Markham in 1986, handles all dealer and customer service for Mitsubishi and Electrohome products.

Since its arrival into the Canadian marketplace, Mitsubishi Electric has been able to offer consumers a wide range of innovative electronic products. Not long ago, for example, wireless remote control for videocassette recorders did not exist. Drawing upon its expertise, Mitsubishi successfully developed this convenient product for VHS videocassette recorders, now an industry standard.

Through revolutionary glass and phosphor technology used to develop color scoreboards for stadiums, Mitsubishi was able to pioneer the Diamond Vision (and Electrohome Blue Optic) picture tube. Widely recognized as a milestone in color television technology, Diamond Vision offers state-of-the-art contrast range.

When the marketplace demanded larger home television sets based on picture tube technology, Mitsubishi was in the forefront, introducing the world's first 37-inch direct-view color television. The company also played an important role in the introduction of cellular telephones to Canada and was one of the first companies to offer portable hand-held cellular telephones.

Mitsubishi Electric Sales Canada Inc.'s famous three-diamond logo appears on a wide range of consumer electronic products. ("Mitsu" means three and "bishi" means diamonds.) But, more important, it identifies a progressive Markham corporate resident that has provided opportunity to numerous individuals, as well as the community as a whole.

ASSINCK BROS. LIMITED

Long before Markham became the corporate centre that it is today, its economic infrastructure was comprised mainly of independently owned businesses. While many such businesses have closed over the years, some have remained open and flourished. An example of such a business is Assinck Bros. Limited.

Established in 1952 by Dutch immigrants Tony and Joe Assinck, the business began as a welding repair shop, located in the vicinity of Old Markham. Following steady growth, the brothers moved the company into its own facility in 1958, which the firm had constructed along Highway 48, just south of Major Mackenzie Road. This location is still the home of Assinck Bros. and its 45 employees.

At the time it moved into its new premises, the company had begun manufacturing equipment for the aggregate industry, which included conveyor systems and steel bins used at sand pits and gravel quarries. With Markham situated on the southern fringe of an area possessing an abundance of pits and quarries, Assinck Bros. had found an ideal spot from which it could ship and service its products, as well as stay in touch with its customers.

During the years that ensued, the company increased its product lines and developed a reputation for quality within the aggregate indus-

try, which relies on efficient and durable machinery, as mechanical breakdowns will cause a halt in operations.

At present Assinck Bros.' product lines include ready-mix cement plants, complete with hoppers, conveyors, and storage bins; topsoil shredders, which pulverize and sift topsoil for lawn and garden use; cold feed systems, which gauge different grades of sand and stone for manufacture of asphalt; screening plants, which separate sand and stone for stockpiling; crushing plants, which break up rocks into crushed stone; and stationary and

portable conveyor systems.

The company often manufactures custom-designed machinery, which entails surveying the physical environment of a pit or quarry, assessing its aggregate composition, and determining production capacity needs. As well, it produces spare parts for its products (of which most contain 90-percent Canadian content) and provides on-site installation and service. It is one of the few companies in its field that offers such a full range of products and services.

When Joe and Tony Assinck retired in 1978 and 1984, respectively, they ensured their business would remain in caring and competent hands by offering company shares to interested employees. Initially 10 employees bought varying levels of ownership in the business. While the number of shareholders has been reduced by attrition, six of seven present owners have worked for the firm for at least 15 years.

The fact that Assinck Bros. Limited operates as a corporate partnership in the truest sense is no doubt a major reason why it has maintained its reputation for quality and dependability, and been a part of Markham's business community for so long.

ALPINE ELECTRONICS OF CANADA, INC.

The year 1989 marked two important milestones in the history of Alpine Electronics of Canada, Inc. The company not only celebrated its 10th anniversary as a corporate entity, but also as a corporate citizen of Markham.

A subsidiary of Japanese-based Alps Electric Company, Alpine Electronics is primarily known for the high-end Alpine mobile audio products it markets and distributes to more than 300 dealer outlets across Canada. But it does the same with Luxman home audio equipment, as well as Alpine mobile cellular phones and security products. An important reason why the firm's mobile and home audio products have earned a reputation for quality in a relatively brief period of time is due to the manufacturing philosophy of its corporate parent.

As the world's largest electronic components manufacturer, Alps Electric uses its own products in the pro-

Alpine's 5952, the world's smallest automotive CD changer.

Alex Romanov, senior vice-president and general manager.

duction of Alpine and Luxman equipment. Its approach, while not usually the norm in the consumer audio industry, allows for the use of leading-edge proprietary technology and ensures optimum quality control.

Closer to home, Alpine Electronics has played an instrumental role in enabling its products to have a significant impact in the Canadian marketplace. It strives to ensure that its retail customers obtain the highest level of product knowledge so that they can make a sound and educated purchase. To achieve this goal, the company places stringent criteria in the selection of its retail dealers. Its dealers are predominantly high-fidelity specialists, independently owned stereo outlets, and small audio chains—all possessing a high degree of professionalism and product expertise.

In the case of Alpine audio equipment, dealers are given

thorough product orientation so that they can assist customers to select the best-possible combination of components to suit the specific audio environment of their vehicle. Because expert installation is crucial to the performance of a mobile audio system, all Alpine dealers must have the ability to offer this service in a highly competent manner. In addition, so customers receive an optimum level of selection, dealers are supplied with the full line of Alpine audio products.

The impressive growth that has enabled Alpine Electronics to become a leader in the Canadian mobile and home audio marketplace has been mirrored by the firm's corporate evolution in Markham. Its first Canadian head office was housed in a 4,300-square-foot facility. Four years later came the move to a 20,000-square-foot premises, followed by the 1987 relocation to its present site on Alden Street, which is three times larger. And, considering its track record, it would not come as a surprise if Alpine Electronics of Canada, Inc., gets a new Markham address before its 20th anniversary in 1999.

HANNA PAPER FIBRES LTD.

By supplying pulp and paper mills with wastepaper used in the manufacture of recycled paper products, Markham's Hanna Paper Fibres Ltd. has been able to provide essential off-shoot benefits to the natural environment, as well as its suppliers and clientele. In the process the company has become Ontario's largest independent wastepaper dealer.

Due to dwindling natural resources and rising raw-material costs, paper producers have had to turn increasingly toward recycled paper. In reducing reliance on raw pulp, Hanna Paper Fibres has played a key role not only in providing a cost-effective industry alternative, but also in the preservation of precious forest lands. Another environmental benefit that stems from the company's business is that countless tons of wastepaper destined for garbage dumps and incinerators end up being recycled into paper products ranging from tissue paper to cardboard packaging. This results in less pollution of the land and air. For businesses that generate large quantities of wastepaper, especially printing companies and financial institutions, Hanna Paper Fibres is able to reduce waste collection and hauling costs, while at the same

The owners of Hanna Paper Fibres Ltd. are (from left) James M. Millar, George Millar, Jr., Lawrence Burns, and George I. Millar, Sr.

time providing financial disbursement for the material it collects.

Hanna Paper Fibres was formed in 1977 by Larry Burns and George Millar, who came to know each other through their former professions. Burns had worked in the printing industry, while Millar had been employed in the waste-recycling business. Both men believed that paper recycling offered a perfect opportunity to start their own business.

When Hanna Paper Fibres opened, it operated from a facility in an old industrial area near downtown Toronto. The firm started with about 10 employees, using several small baling machines to compact and bale the wastepaper it collected from numerous businesses in the Metro Toronto area. Incidentally, the company's name was derived from the street it was located on—Hanna Avenue.

In two brief years following its inception, Hanna Paper Fibres outgrew its original premises and moved to Markham. Its plant on John Street proved an ideal location in that it enabled the firm to provide better service to many of its clients who had relocated or were planning to relocate to Markham. In addition, the location gave the company more direct and less traffic-congested access to its numerous clients outside downtown Toronto.

Using larger and more sophisticated machinery at its Markham location, Hanna Paper Fibres grew dramatically. In 1984 Burns and Millar opened Hanna Paper Recycling Inc. in Boston, and Missis-

Hanna operates a large fleet of trucks serving printers and paper mills in Canada and New England.

High-production balers can package 20 tons per hour of recyclable wastepaper and shredded office records.

sauga Paper Fibres Ltd. in Mississauga, Ontario. The following year the Markham operation moved into its own, newly constructed premises on Addiscott Court.

In order to collect wastepaper from its suppliers, Hanna Paper Fibres deploys its own fleet of tractor-trailer trucks and relies on three different methods of collection. The company supplies large generators of wastepaper with compactors and/or baling machines, resulting in either compacted or prebaled material, or both. Moderate-volume suppliers usually receive bins in which different stocks of paper are loosely sorted. Lastly, material is also supplied by paper dealers and independent haulers who collect wastepaper from smaller-size producers.

All recycled paper that Hanna Paper Fibres sends to paper mills worldwide is compacted under 300 tons of pressure, baled, and then wired. Separating different types of paper is an essential process due to the fact that paper mills all have very specific wastepaper requirements. These are based on the chemical processes they rely on to break down wastepaper and produce it

into recycled paper products, along with the type of equipment they use. Staples and plastic bindings must all be eradicated to ensure high levels of purity. The types of wastepaper that Hanna Paper Fibres collects is strictly of a high-grade variety and includes letterhead, envelopes, pages from books, and other similar types of printing paper. The company also collects foil paper, comprised mainly of food packaging, from which tin foil is later separated through a smelting process.

To complement its paper collections service, Hanna Paper Fibres operates a confidential paper-shredding service that is used by clients consisting mainly of financial institutions, insurance companies, and government agencies. Bonded employees supervise the shredding process, which occurs in a self-contained and specially secured section of the firm's plant. Once the shredding is completed clients are provided with certificates of destruction, while shredded material is often recycled.

As a corporate resident of Markham that is a key player in an emerging and environmentally conscientious industry, Hanna Paper Fibres continually strives to encourage and educate the local community to collect wastepaper for recycling. To accomplish this, the company is active with many community recycling groups and local government recycling efforts, as well as various youth organizations and school groups. In addition, the firm conducts ongoing tours of its plant in order to promote recycling.

In moving its operation to Markham to accommodate its growth and to provide an optimum-level service to its clientele, Hanna Paper Fibres Ltd. has achieved something even more important. It has helped the community play a greater role in the preservation of the planet's diminishing natural resources.

The newly built head office of Hanna Paper Fibres Ltd. is located at 70 Addiscott Court in Markham.

OE INC.

"Markham? Why that's halfway to the country cottage!" That was the response of some employees when, many years ago, the news reached them that OE Inc. was moving its downtown Toronto offices to a new location in an area northeast of the city known as Markham. Once established in Markham, however, opinions soon changed, and the infectious enthusiasm of the district became evident as, like members of the same family, OE and Markham rapidly grew up together. The affinity between the two was greatly enhanced by the fact that OE soon became one of Markham's larger employers. Today, as Markham continues to grow, so does OE—to a future that gives every indication of ongoing mutual prosperity.

OE was founded in 1906 and made public in 1985, trading on the Montreal and Toronto stock exchanges. The company has four main operating divisions: business machines, furniture, wholesale, and leasing. OE operates from six branches: Montreal, Quebec City, Ottawa, Calgary, Hamilton, and Toronto. The company's Toronto branch at Markham is by far the largest OE operation in Canada, with a modern 152,000-square-foot building on Denison Street. It houses sales, service, administration, warehouse, and retailer training functions. Even though OE is primarily a distributor and wholesaler of office equipment, the building also includes a retail outlet, one of many that the company operates within its extensive branch territories. A second sizable building, also located on Denison Street, houses OE's large and progressive office furniture operation.

Supplementing the company's direct sales force is its Wholesale Division, which provides customers with exclusive product lines through hundreds of retail dealers nationwide. These independent dealers operate in communities not serviced by OE's main offices.

The OE corporate management style keeps the company in pace

Michael Devitt, president of OE Inc.

with modern innovations and has earned it many distinctions, including that of being North America's largest office equipment company and the world's largest distributor of Canon copiers. It also firmly established the company in the *Financial Post*'s top 500 businesses in Canada.

In a period extending over 80 years of supplying Canada's business community with top-name equipment and office furniture, OE has always been a leader. What has been the key to the firm's continuous success? The answer comes from OE's president, T. Michael Devitt, "Customer service is the key to our success. Once you give that comfort level to the customer, he comes to you for a lot of product."

As product sales expand so does the market for supplies and peripheral equipment. The company has positioned itself to take full advantage of this opportunity not only by augmenting its telemarketing operation but by establishing a research and development operation within the organization to guarantee top quality in supplies and accessories.

OE also established the Leasing Division with improved customer service in mind. As leases and rentals are controlled by the company the lessee may upgrade at any time without penalty, provided, of course, that the replace-

ment is obtained from OE.

Says Devitt, "Today you're dealing with a very knowledgeable buyer who needs that comfort level with the product." As a result, he insists that OE sales personnel should be thoroughly educated to fully understand the product that they sell. To back this efficient sales staff, skilled technicians, service personnel, and sales support specialists are required to assure sales and after-sales support for the customer. OE guarantees the continuance of this policy by providing specialized training in these fields also.

The firm's corporate management is quick to realize that all the product and technical training in the world will not provide the complete key to continued overall company success if the proper esprit de corps is not maintained throughout the entire organization. OE's president points out, "We think one of the key things in any business is to

have fun, and we try to ensure our employees enjoy the job." As a result of this philosophy, the firm has attracted excellent marketing, sales, and service people.

To ensure continued loyalty to the company, OE's corporate management offers many excellent incentives to its staff, including an employee share option plan. Income capacity for sales personnel is not subject to a ceiling, resulting in a highly motivated sales staff with top-dollar income opportunities. High-achieving sales people are well rewarded by such arrangements as expense-paid incentive trips through OE's Director's Club. Another OE policy advocates promotion of employees from within the corporate structure to management positions wherever possible, rather than hiring from outside the firm. The family spirit is kept alive by the encouragement of company social and sporting events from the corpo-

An artist's rendering of OE Inc.'s main building at 1490 Denison Street in Markham.

rate level, and this, in no small measure, contributes to the overall success of staff motivation, creating a built-in vibrant spirit of co-operation throughout the entire organization.

All these factors—solid management practices, a motivated sales force, a smooth-running support organization assisted by the latest advances in office technology, top-name quality products, and good customer service—ensure OE's sustained future growth. As Canadian companies continue to increase their investment in fixed assets and Markham itself continues to expand as a major centre of corporate concentration, OE Inc.'s board of directors anticipates that the firm's growth will continue, especially in Markham.

HYUNDAI AUTO CANADA INC.

In order to become a prominent and respected participant in the Canadian auto industry, Hyundai Auto Canada Inc. has invested some $500 million into its Canadian operations since it was formed in 1983.

Its main facilities include a head office/parts distribution centre in Markham; an aluminum wheel manufacturing plant in nearby Newmarket; a vehicle assembly plant in Bromont, Quebec; and a parts distribution centre in Vancouver.

The company chose Markham as the site for its head office/parts distribution centre for several reasons. Not only did the area offer quick accessibility to major transport routes, it also contained a skilled labor force with experience in all aspects of the auto industry. As well, Hyundai believed that the progressive nature of Markham's business environment would complement its operation.

More than 180 employees work at Hyundai's Markham facility, which opened in 1987 and has 220,000 square feet of warehouse and administrative space. The parts distribution centre serves a network

of 170 Hyundai dealerships across Canada (which has grown from an initial network of 48 dealerships), and annually sources about $25 million worth of various Canadian-made auto parts to its parent firm, Hyundai Motor Company of South Korea. Ranging from tires and glass to spark plugs and carpets, the parts are used in the manufacture of vehicles destined for export to Canada and are part of the company's mandate to increase the Canadian content of vehicles sold to the Canadian marketplace.

Hyundai's parts distribution centre in Markham stocks a full inventory of parts for all present and past Hyundai models. In order to improve customer service at the dealership level, a computerized inventory order system instantly informs dealers of the availability of any given part, and also specifies delivery dates and back orders.

Once Hyundai began selling cars to the Canadian marketplace in

Hyundai Auto Canada Inc. corporate headquarters in Markham.

1984, it experienced virtually instant fame. Its Pony sold more than 25,000 units and proved to be the most successful launch of a new model import vehicle in Canadian history. The following year Hyundai introduced the Stellar compact sedan, and sales were again overwhelming. With more than 79,000 units sold, Hyundai was the number-one-selling import car company in Canada that year.

The corporate philosophy of Hyundai is to build automobiles that satisfy human needs and offer outstanding value at an affordable price. To attain this goal, the firm uses a combination of modern research and time-tested ideas. At the same time Hyundai is dedicated to fostering mutually beneficial economic relationships in each of the more than 60 countries where its vehicles are sold.

On a more modest but equally important level, Hyundai Auto Canada Inc. and the community of Markham have entered into their own mutually rewarding relationship—exemplified by their progressive attitude and desire for excellence.

Photo by Dawn Goss

Business and Professions

Greater Markham's business and professional community brings a wealth of service, ability, and insight to the area.

Photo by J. Holman

THE MARKHAM BOARD OF TRADE

Incorporated under the Board of Trade Act in 1981, The Markham Board of Trade has had remarkable success in its efforts to support and promote local business. Its membership base, which originally consisted of 30 corporate concerns, has grown to a present size of more than 1,000. In addition, a considerable number of businesses located outside of Markham, but that conduct business in the community, are also members.

Large and small firms alike have benefited from being members of The Markham Board of Trade. Using its various meetings and functions as a forum for interaction, they are better able to offer their resources as support to one another—leading to new paths for mutual growth and co-operation. In order to facilitate networking between members, The Markham Board of Trade holds monthly meetings featuring prominent speakers, trade shows in which members display

Karen Mugford delivers the president's message after her inauguration in June 1988.

their products and services, various social events, and an annual golf tournament.

As part of its official mandate, which states: "We are responsive to the collective needs of our members and promote the economic and social prosperity of our community,"

Markham Mayor Tony Roman, president Graham Nichols, and Don Cousens, MPP, officially open the Board's office in May 1988.

The Markham Board of Trade plays an active role in educating and informing its members. Especially useful for small businesses, which often lack the information resources of larger firms, are regular educational seminars on topics such as the effects of changing government legislation on business, credit and collections, office automation, management practices, and human relations.

Another service to the business community is the Business Self-Help Office that opened in January 1990. Managed in co-operation with the Town of Markham and the Ontario Ministry of Industry, Trade and Technology, the resource centre offers both information and consulting services.

As well, The Markham Board of Trade offers a business resource centre containing information from its own data base and various government branches, in addition to a monthly newsletter, membership directory and buyers' guide, business re-

United States, Europe, and the Pacific Rim. This arrangement provides for information, training, and technology exchanges, as well as ongoing trade missions.

Funded mainly through membership fees and fund-raising projects, The Markham Board of Trade is governed by a volunteer board of directors that is elected by its members. Various committees comprised of volunteers are responsible for implementing programs and objectives, while a paid, full-time staff conducts day-to-day functions.

As the town of Markham continues its rapid pace of commercial/industrial development, The Markham Board of Trade anticipates its membership will double by the end of 1992, to approximately 2,500 firms. More important, its ever-growing number of members proves that local businesses, large and small, view mutual support and interaction as a key ingredient in their pursuit of growth and prosperity.

Left: The board's premises are located on the ninth floor, which also houses the Markham Business Self-Help Office.

Below: Pictured here (from left) are Lisa Ash, receptionist/secretary; (standing) Vanda Gayowsky, executive assistant; and Ethel Luhtanen, executive director.

ferral service, membership lists, and mailing labels. It also strives to represent its members' business interests and concerns to government and the media.

For member firms The Markham Board of Trade has joined forces with more than 300 other boards of trade and chambers of commerce across Canada to provide a cost-effective group insurance plan. Available coverage includes various forms of life and disability insurance, along with extended health and dental plans.

On the international front, The Markham Board of Trade, in conjunction with the Town of Markham, is launching twinning programs with compatible municipalities in the

TOWN OF MARKHAM

In the service industry, Markham is home to American Express Canada, Allstate Insurance Co. of Canada, A.C. Nielsen Company of Canada, and electronic data centres for two of Canada's largest banks—

Left: The A.C. Nielsen Company of Canada found that its move to Markham was an excellent decision.

Below: American Express Canada, Inc., one of the many corporate headquarters located in Markham.

Markham Township was surveyed and initially settled in the 1790s. It was named after William Markham, Archbishop of York, England, and friend of John Graves Simcoe, Upper Canada's first lieutenant-governor.

The fertile land surrounding the villages of Markham and Unionville, which was once the bottom of a shallow lake, offered prime agricultural opportunities for English, French, German, Scottish, and Irish immigrants. While farming is still a major business in the municipality, it is industrial and commercial development that has fueled Markham's recent and unprecedented growth, transforming it into one of Canada's most vibrant communities.

Since 1971 Markham's population has almost quintupled from approximately 36,000 to more than 150,000. More important, the creation of new jobs within the 83-square-mile municipality has actually surpassed the rate of population growth. Some 5,000 various-size businesses employ more than 60,000 people, compared with about 11,000 employment opportunities that existed in 1971. Projections indicate that by the year 2000 Markham's population will surpass 175,000, and that the number of employment opportunities will reach 100,000.

A common characteristic of the many firms that have their Canadian headquarters in Markham is that they are involved in advanced technology or are service oriented. Those in computer- and high-technology-related fields include IBM Canada, Apple Canada, Semitech Microelectronics, Olivetti Canada, Sun Microsystems Canada, Memorex Canada, Tie/Communications Canada, GEAC, Ford Electronics Manufacturing, Johnson Controls, and Fisher Scientific.

Markham-based companies that rely on high technology to produce other products include automotive parts manufacturer Magna International, photographic supplier and processor Black Photo Corporation, chemical producer Cyanamid Canada, office furniture maker Steelcase Canada, and clothing manufacturer Levi Strauss & Co. (Canada).

Scotiabank and the Canadian Imperial Bank of Commerce.

Increasingly, Markham is also a popular choice for firms from the Far East seeking opportunities in Canada's commercial heartland of Ontario. Hyundai, the Korean automaking giant, recently built a massive parts distribution centre in Markham. Other Far Eastern companies located in the municipality include Samsung Electronics of Canada, Toshiba of Canada, Kubota Tractor Canada, and Mitsubishi Electric Sales Canada.

There are several reasons why Markham has attracted so many quality businesses. Situated on the northern boundary of Metro Toronto, the municipality is located in proximity to Canada's largest concentration of people and purchasing power. Furthermore, it lies within a day's drive of the central and northeastern United States, which has a market of 120 million people.

Markham offers businesses quick access to road, rail, air, and water transportation routes. It is minutes from Highway 401, which spans southern Ontario from Windsor to Montreal, Quebec. Major east-west lines of Canada's transcontinental railway system are equally close, as are three commercial airports.

Located in the heart of Markham, Toronto-Buttonville International Airport specializes in private and commercial flights. Home to more than 300 aircraft, it is Canada's largest privately owned airport. Pearson International Airport and Toronto Island Airport are both about a half-hour drive from Markham—as is the Port of Toronto, which can provide waterway access to virtually anywhere in the world.

Due to a steadily growing and well-balanced residential and commercial/industrial tax base, Markham's residents and businesses pay among the lowest tax rates in the Metro Toronto area. The municipality's commercial growth has also enabled it to reduce the balance of residential to commercial tax assessment from a ratio of 81:19 in 1971

Markham offers big-city living in a country setting.

to 72:28 in 1988. The remarkable growth of commercial investment in Markham is further shown by the soaring value of industrial building permits issued, from $45 million in 1983 to $242 million in 1988. With an abundance of competitively priced land designated for commercial/industrial development, Markham offers a natural location for most businesses.

Another reason for Markham's low tax rate is that its local government has practised sound fiscal management and controlled borrowing. The municipality built more than $50 million worth of libraries, recreation centres, parks, and a professional theatre between 1979 and 1988—without going into debt.

Significant projects undertaken in recent years to improve the quality of living in the town include beautification of Old Markham Village; restoration of downtown Unionville; Mount Joy Community Centre, an athletic complex; construction of li-

The Markham Museum features the oldest church in Markham, a diesel-powered sawmill, a steam-driven cider mill, and the Acadia, a rail car used by five Canadian prime ministers.

braries in the Thornhill and Milliken areas; and the new Markham Civic Centre.

Demographically, Markham possesses a well-educated and skilled labor force. Many of its residents work for businesses in the community, and their earning power is reflected in the fact that Markham ranks consistently as one of Canada's highest income per capita areas. In terms of residential growth, the municipality has averaged about 2,000 new housing units annually for the past several years.

During the 1990s Markham's growth is expected to slow somewhat, as available tracts of serviced land are fully developed. At that time the Town of Markham and the province of Ontario will have to decide whether it is in the best interest of the community to service more land for development.

Whatever the future may hold, Markham has come a long way from its sleepy, rural roots, and is a shining example of a community where people and business have grown side by side.

BLAKE, CASSELS & GRAYDON

Blake, Cassels & Graydon is one of Canada's oldest and largest law firms, and has been a prominent member of Toronto's business community for more than a century. It was founded in 1856 by the Honorable Edward Blake, who went on to become the Premier of Ontario, and later, the Minister of Justice for Canada.

Blakes, long recognized for its professionalism and expertise in all facets of law, is a progressive firm, with an entrepreneurial outlook. The significant growth of the firm's practice over the years has been a contributing factor in its expansion into major financial centres in Canada and abroad.

In 1987 Blakes recognized the rapid growth and development of Markham as a major centre for large and growing Canadian and multinational companies. In response to the need for an accessible, full-service law office in the area, Blakes established a fully staffed, self-sufficient office, conveniently situated at Highway 404 and Highway 7.

The firm has brought the expertise and experience of a large downtown law firm to the Markham area, thus enabling local clients to benefit from the available services, technology, and contacts of a large, established firm. Although Blakes' York

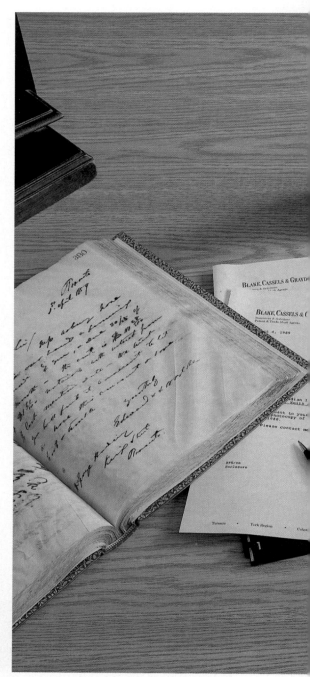

Region office provides many specialized services that are attractive to Markham's large corporate concerns, the office also provides the basic corporate and commercial services required by the small and medium-size businesses that are the driving force behind the growth of the community.

Some of the services provided by the York Region office include corporate and commercial law, real

tions contracts, patents, copyrights, trade secrets, electronic banking, and electronic publishing.

Blakes' expertise in providing general corporate services extends from routine business transactions to complex mergers and acquisitions. The firm also advises clients in the financial services industry, including Canadian chartered banks, trust companies, a number of foreign banks, and several security dealers.

The York Region office addresses all of these needs with more than 50 professional and support staff, and is fully computerized for maximum efficiency. It also has the support of more than 800 people at the main office in Toronto as well as offices in Ottawa, Vancouver, Calgary, and London, England. These additional offices provide the opportunity for local clients to take advantage of the firm's experience, resources, and contacts, and also ensures timely and cost-effective service for all clients, whether they are local, regional, national, or multinational.

The firm's lawyers also take an active interest in the community. The York Region office is a strong supporter of The Markham Board of Trade, Markham Theatre, York Symphony, and other local cultural groups. Individual members of the firm devote considerable time to teaching and writing about law, as well as to local charities, sports, and cultural groups. One of the lawyers regularly contributes a column to a local newspaper.

The recent growth of the York Region office, in terms of professional staff and services provided, is a reflection of the strong emphasis Blake, Cassels & Graydon has always placed on serving the needs of its clients. As a part of one of the largest law firms in Canada, the York Region office has maintained the firm's reputation for top-quality legal work, provided with a practical business approach and a personal touch.

estate, land development and planning, financial services, civil litigation, administrative law, intellectual property, foreign investment, mergers and acquisitions, oil and gas, estates and immigration, insolvency, taxation, and labor and employment.

When Blakes established its office in York Region, the firm paid careful attention to the legal needs of this dynamic community. For example, there was an obvious need for lawyers with expertise in all aspects of real estate law from the sale of vacant land, through the municipal planning process, to complex development and construction projects.

The York Region office also has a strong focus on high-technology law, and provides current and timely advice on technology licensing, international technology transfers, computer sales and acquisi-

PETROFF PARTNERSHIP ARCHITECTS

Willowdale office to a more spacious environment in the Markham Executive Centre near Highway 7 and Warden Avenue. In addition to being designed by the firm, the four-building complex is also being developed by Petroff Partnership Architects and is a reflection of the firm's confidence in continued commercial prosperity for the community. (The final stage of the centre is slated for completion in 1994.)

With a staff of 120, Petroff Partnership Architects brings a diversity of individual and collective

Left: The AT&T head office building in North York, Ontario.

Below: Petroff Partnership Architects' reception area in Markham.

Specializing in the design of commercial buildings and shopping centres, Markham's Petroff Partnership Architects is one of Canada's largest and most reputable architectural firms. Examples of its outstanding design work abound from coast to coast, being particularly evident across southern Ontario. In fact, it is highly likely that most southern Ontarians have, at one time or another, shopped inside at least one of the many malls, department stores, and supermarkets designed by the firm.

Locally, notable projects designed by Petroff Partnership Architects include Markville Town Centre and Markham Square shopping centres, the Markham Executive Centre office building complex, and the Mayfair racquet clubs. Other nearby examples are the AT&T head office building in Willowdale, Observatory Place in Richmond Hill, Upper Canada Mall in Newmarket, and Simpsons and The Bay department stores in North York's Fairview Mall.

Founded in 1957 by Henry Petroff, the firm quickly established itself as an industry pioneer, designing suburban shopping centres,

multi-storey residential buildings, and mixed-use office/retail complexes that emerged in the late 1950s and early 1960s. As the scope of these projects grew in size and sophistication, the firm was able to develop its expertise and experience and eventually enter the forefront of commercial building design.

As a result of the steady growth that followed, Petroff Partnership Architects became a corporate resident of Markham in 1988, moving from its longtime

talents to each new project it undertakes. No matter the magnitude or complexity of a project, the organization's clients are assured of proven expertise, which includes accurate budgeting and scheduling along with a minimum of unexpected construction difficulties. In addition, the firm utilizes a team-oriented approach to design in which each phase of a project is managed by a group of in-house specialists.

A major project can involve as

many as 30 professionals, working
in five- to eight-person teams on individual components of the project.
The project manager is usually one
of the firm's partners or associates,
whose responsibilities include client
relations and general co-ordination.
Other key personnel include assistant project managers, designers,
draftsmen, resource staff, and field
inspectors.

Designers are responsible for
the initial conceptual design of a project as well as renderings and models. Draftsmen, who compose the
bulk of the firm's staff, create working drawings, often through the use
of computer-assisted design equipment. Resource staff functions involve writing project specifications,
investigating new construction materials and systems, determining contrac-
tual legalities and obligations, and
maintaining a comprehensive library of construction materials and
products. Field inspectors visit work
during construction and monitor quality and progress.

Because teamwork is such a
vital aspect of the service Petroff
Partnership Architects provides to its
clients, the firm strives to foster an
amicable, family-type atmosphere so
that its staff can function effectively
and in harmony. The organization's

partners and associates have an
open-door policy with all employees
and maintain personal working relationships with everyone. The firm
publishes a regular newsletter, hosts
numerous social gatherings for its
staff, and supports and sponsors
employee baseball, basketball, and
golf activities.

The design philosophy of
Petroff Partnership Architects offers
commercial investors the assurance
that the firm's work is directed
toward long-term aesthetic and functional value, thereby providing maximum returns on investment for
many years to come. The firm empha-
sizes to its clients that design sensitivity is essential to establishing a
corporate or commercial complex
that will appeal to today's discriminat-
ing users. However, its commitment
to superior and sensible design is
balanced by architectural solutions
that are tailored to clients' financial
realities.

The soundness of this principle
has enabled Petroff Partnership
Architects to nurture lasting professional relationships with some of
Canada's largest developers, including Burnac Leaseholds, Cadillac

Fairview Corporation, Cambridge
Shopping Centres, Campeau Corporation, Hudson's Bay Company, J.D.S.
Investments, Marathon Realty,
Markborough Properties, Menkes Developments, Morguard Investments,
and Tridel Corporation.

An important contributor to the
changing face of Markham, Petroff
Partnership Architects is a firm that
truly views the present with an eye
to the future.

PEAT MARWICK THORNE

As the Canadian arm of the world's largest public accounting and management consulting firm, Peat Marwick Thorne has the distinction of being the first major international firm of its kind to open an office in Markham. It is a decision that reflects the organization's commitment to serve the many businesses that in recent years have established operations in the community.

The firm's Markham office opened in 1985, one year before Peat Marwick International merged with Dutch-based Klynveld Main Goerdler. Under this corporate structure, Peat Marwick Thorne's Canadian operation is owned and operated by its Canadian partners. But, as an integral part of Klynveld Peat Marwick Goerdler (KPMG), it is able to offer its clients knowledgeable and innovative services worldwide. This benefits Canadian organizations with foreign operations, as well as those seeking to expand their opportunities abroad. Conversely, the same principle applies to foreign companies.

The KPMG network is comprised of more than 5,000 partners and 43,000 professional staff based

in more than 115 countries. In Canada, Peat Marwick Thorne operates offices in 61 communities from coast to coast. At the end of 1989 the Markham office possessed the collective expertise of five partners and 50 professional staff.

Peat Marwick Thorne Chartered Accountants and Peat Marwick Stevenson & Kellogg Management Consultants were formed in September 1989 as a result of a merger of two of Canada's leading professional services firms.

The merger of Peat Marwick and Thorne Ernst & Whinney and

Peat Marwick Consulting Group and Stevenson Kellogg Ernst & Whinney has resulted in the creation of Canada's largest firm of professional business advisers. Peat Marwick Thorne and Peat Marwick Stevenson & Kellogg has more than 800 partners and a total staff of more than 5,600 nationwide.

The first Peat Marwick office to open in Canada was in Winnipeg in 1907. Very quickly offices were established in Montreal, Vancouver, Toronto, and Calgary. The Peat Marwick firm in Canada prospered and grew during the postwar years with several mergers enhancing the firm's geographic coverage. The management consulting practice was formally established in 1954.

Thorne Ernst & Whinney was formed in 1986 by the merger in Canada of Thorne Riddell and Ernst & Whinney. Stevenson Kellogg Ernst & Whinney was founded in 1936 as Stevenson & Kellogg. Thorne Stevenson & Kellogg was formed in 1980 and joined in the 1986 merger to become Stevenson Kellogg Ernst & Whinney.

The combined resources of the new firm will allow clients of Peat Marwick Thorne to benefit from in-

The private business advisory services group.

vestments in new products and services designed to meet its clients' expanding needs.

While Peat Marwick Thorne was devoted to providing mainly auditing services in its early years, its present scope of expertise has grown to include a host of other financial and consulting services. The firm's Markham office, for example, is organized into four groups of practice: auditing, taxation, business advisory services, and financial advisory services.

The audit group, the largest in the office, specializes in accounting and auditing services, as well as advice in financing, business acquisitions, and securities regulation. The client portfolio of the audit group is mainly mid- to large-size public and private businesses.

The cornerstone of the taxation group is tax-planning advice and preparation of tax returns for corporations and individuals. Its other areas of tax expertise range from personal financial planning and corporate reorganizations to international investment and trading activities. Since Peat Marwick Thorne is part of the KPMG global network, its clients benefit from the firm's immediate access to expert advice on tax

systems anywhere in the world.

Working hand in hand with the many small- to mid-size businesses in the local area, the business advisory group specializes in matters that are crucial to this sector. This includes development of bookkeeping and accounting systems, business planning and management, and microcomputer systems consulting.

The financial advisory services group includes the provision of service for corporate reorganization and insolvency, business valuations, mergers, acquisitions, and corporate finance. A substantial portion of the assignments of this practice involve conducting assessment and monitoring engagements for secured lenders, and acting as a consultant to financially troubled companies.

By drawing upon the expertise

The tax group.

of professionals at its downtown Toronto office, Peat Marwick Thorne's Markham practice can also assist clients in areas such as corporate mergers, economic impact studies, executive recruitment, large-scale information-processing systems, and forensic accounting. The forensic group utilizes its investigative skills and experience in matters concerning corporate investigations, litigation accounting, criminal cases, insurance claims, and government inquiries.

With its decision to come to Markham, Peat Marwick Thorne has displayed a high level of business initiative, as well as confidence in the expertise of its people and the local business community. No doubt, these are attributes that have contributed to make the firm a leader in its field at all levels of business.

The audit group.

DELOITTE & TOUCHE

The reasons behind the opening of the first office bearing the Deloitte name in Canada in 1912 are much the same as those behind the recent opening of the Deloitte & Touche office in Markham.

British based and known as Deloitte, Plender, Griffiths & Co. at the time, the firm chose Montreal as the location to establish its roots on Canadian soil. Expanding industrially and commercially, the city was the country's financial centre and offered the firm an ideal springboard into the Canadian business world. Among its early clients was

the Imperial Tobacco Company of Canada, which obtained its charter the same year and is still a client today. A second location, in Vancouver, operated from 1912 to 1920 and served clients such as Dominion Sawmills and Lumber Co. in Revelstoke, British Columbia. In 1954 the firm became an autonomous Canadian partnership with the merger of Deloitte, Plender, Haskins & Sells and Winnipeg-based Millar, Macdonald & Co.

Early in 1990, in response to the changing needs of its clients carrying on business in an increasingly complex global marketplace, Deloitte Haskins & Sells and Touche Ross combined their resources to form Deloitte & Touche. The firm's decision to open a Markham office in 1989 was based on both the opportunity to provide optimum service to its clients and a sound business plan for the future. Located in the Valleywood Corporate Centre at the major intersection of highways 404 and 7, the office functions as a con-

venient service base for clients in York Region and northern Metro Toronto. At the same time Markham, as one of Canada's most rapidly growing commercial/industrial centres, offers Deloitte & Touche a prime opportunity to expand its clientele— just as Montreal did in the early 1900s. The firm's commitment to serve local businesses and individuals, and develop a strong presence in the community is further evidenced by the fact that it employs more than 75 professional and support staff at its Markham location.

Deloitte & Touche is among Canada's largest public accounting firms, with more than 80 offices from coast to coast employing in excess of 4,800 professional and support staff. And Deloitte & Touche can help its clients do business in the global marketplace through a sophisticated network of member firms and international contacts in more than 100 countries.

As the world of business and finance has and continues to become

Some of the partners and managers in Deloitte & Touche's Markham office assembled outside their new home at the Valleywood Corporate Center, a project of the firm's client Inducon Development Corporation. Seen here are (from left) John Budd, Jim Chwartacky, Sid Disenhouse, Loraine McIntosh, Paul George, Bob McLeod, Jane McGowan, Shelly Dale, Joe Watson (vice-president/Inducon), Ken Villiers (vice-president/Inducon), and Drew Gerrard.

Owner/managers, such as Shirley Rad-bourne, depend on Deloitte & Touche for personalized service and sound advice. Gathered behind Shirley on the porch of her popular women's clothing shop—11 Joseph Fashions—are (from left) Drew Gerrard (partner), Ron McNeill (managing partner), and Shirley's husband, Bill Jackson.

more complex, Deloitte & Touche's role has evolved from traditional auditor to that of creative business adviser.

As a creative business adviser, Deloitte & Touche has developed a multidisciplinary approach that includes auditing, accounting, and taxation, as well as management consulting, computer services, and credit counselling. These services are mixed and matched to make sure clients receive comprehensive advice tailored to their individual needs. The approach ensures a proper allocation of skills to each of the many situations D&T professionals may encounter, whether related to business growth and finance, management and systems improvement,

or interim management and business wind-up.

The firm's commitment to develop better ways to service its clientele is demonstrated by the computer programs it has designed to enable clients to take advantage of business information so they can reduce operating costs, improve productivity, and obtain more effective planning and control.

For example, the firm's automated audit technique uses microcomputers to significantly enhance the delivery speed, quality, flexibility, and value of the accounting and financial analysis services that Deloitte & Touche provides its clients. The firm will also ensure that clients have the right level of security over computer-held information—too little and they are exposed, too much and it gets in the way of day-to-day operations.

As another example of its hands-on practical advice, D&T has developed a training program to help businesses of any size take full advantage of today's desk-top computers. Businesses, from plastics manufacturers to flower shops, are enjoying the efficiency of computerized accounting and office management, simply by ensuring that their staff have the best business computer training.

In the Markham area, Deloitte & Touche serves a wide range of

corporate clients, with particular emphasis on high-technology and service-sector firms, financial institutions, non-profit organizations, car dealerships, and owner-managed businesses.

As a part of its commitment to provide quality service, Deloitte & Touche consistently adheres to practices that enable it to attract and retain professionals who are among the most knowledgeable in their field. This is accomplished by following sound recruiting practices, by recognizing employee initiative and rewarding results, by offering comprehensive development programs, and by providing carefully guided practical experience.

Considering the many different businesses located in Markham and those yet to arrive—all with their own unique circumstances and opportunities—Deloitte & Touche's Markham operation will have its work cut out for many years to come, and undoubtedly will prosper in tandem with the progressive and dynamic community.

The firm's microcomputer consultants tailor systems to the specific needs of each business. Shelly Dale (director/microcomputer services) and Jane McGowan (national director/management training) have put in place microcomputer training courses designed to help Markham businesspeople get the most from their computer investment.

PANNELL KERR MacGILLIVRAY

With corporate roots dating back to 1857, Pannell Kerr MacGillivray is one of Canada's oldest chartered accounting firms. It operates practices in most of the country's principal cities, as well as a number of smaller urban centres, employing a staff of more than 900—which includes approximately 160 partners.

The company's Canadian operation was formed by the 1987 merger of the firms Pannell Kerr Forster and Spicer MacGillivray. Internationally, Pannell Kerr MacGillivray is affiliated with Pannell Kerr Forster Worldwide, a global network of autonomous accounting firms operating in some 80 countries.

Pannell Kerr MacGillivray opened its Markham office in 1981 so it could provide more efficient service to its local clients. In addition, the firm's management believed that a Markham-based practice, rather than its downtown Toronto office, would be better able to grow along with the increasing number of businesses in the area.

Almost a decade later it is clear the rationale for moving to Markham has resulted in success for Pannell Kerr MacGillivray. To meet the needs of its expanding client base, the Markham practice has grown from an initial number of 2 partners and 8 staff members to 5 partners and some 40 staff members. Local clients range in size from multinational corporations to sole proprietorships, and include the Town of Markham and Markham Hydro.

Two areas in which Pannell Kerr MacGillivray possesses extensive expertise are the hospitality and tourism industry and owner-managed businesses. The firm has enabled many business dreams to become a reality and to thrive in subsequent years. It has also assisted countless clients raise equity capital and secure the necessary financing to start up or expand their entrepreneurial ventures.

Realizing that sound financial advice can dramatically influence how quickly and effectively business goals are reached, Pannell Kerr MacGillivray strives to offer clients a full range of services and advice in areas that include auditing, accounting, taxation, securities filings, mergers, acquisitions, valuations, computer consulting, and operations reviews for both corporate and public-sector concerns.

Whether it involves helping a new business get off the ground or developing a strategy for an established firm to respond to a new challenge or opportunity, Pannell Kerr MacGillivray is committed to a personal, accessible, and hands-on approach. This philosophy has evolved from understanding that each client is a unique organization, with unique problems and opportunities.

Ultimately, by seeking to understand clients and their businesses, industries, employees, plans, and goals, Pannell Kerr MacGillivray has been able to serve their needs with the highest level of integrity and objectivity—and remain dedicated to their best interests.

Pannell Kerr MacGillivray is one of Canada's oldest chartered accounting firms. Its clients range in size from multinational corporations to sole proprietorships, and include the Town of Markham and Markham Hydro.

ALLSTATE INSURANCE COMPANIES OF CANADA

From the time the Allstate Centre became the head office of Allstate Insurance Companies of Canada in 1986, it quickly established itself as a Markham landmark. The building's majestic presence and bold design symbolize not only a progressive and prosperous community, but also a company that is a leader and innovator in its field. And like the rapid impact its headquarters has made on the community, Allstate has become one of Canada's most prominent insurance companies in a surprisingly brief period of time.

The firm was founded in 1931 by the United States retail giant Sears, Roebuck and Co. as a vehicle to market insurance products directly to the public. It was not until 1953 that Allstate opened its first Canadian branch office in Toronto. Initially the Canadian subsidiary sold only automobile insurance, but gradually it expanded its product lines to include residential, commercial, liability, and individual or group life and health coverage. In 1964 the operation was incorporated as two separate Canadian entities specializing in general and life insurance, and consequently became known as Allstate Insurance Companies of Canada.

An innovator, Allstate was the first insurance company in Canada to introduce drive-in claim offices to appraise automobile damage, and among the first to computerize customer service records. It has also been a key participant in research to improve highway safety by seeking ways to upgrade automobile protection equipment, as well as campaigning against drinking and driving.

As part of its philosophy, Allstate has strong beliefs about being a responsible corporate citizen. In addition to encouraging employees to participate in local charity and social organizations, the company provides financial assistance to various groups through the Allstate Foundation of Canada. Established in 1977 with a $2-million grant, the foundation donates on a Canada-wide basis, with particular emphasis on safety, education, culture, and charity. Locally Allstate has traditionally been a major supporter of the York Region United Way.

Serving as the head office for Allstate Insurance Companies of Canada, Allstate Centre embodies in its design the progressive nature of the firm and its prominence in the industry.

One of the main reasons for Allstate's success in the marketplace is undoubtedly the high standards it sets in dealing with consumers. Realizing that each customer must be treated as an individual, the firm's commitment is to be fair, responsive, and conduct business with a high level of integrity. It also strives to continuously better inform consumers and offer superior value through innovation.

For more than 1,800 employees across Canada, including the staff of approximately 750 at its Markham head office, Allstate Insurance Companies of Canada provides a professional environment in which they can realize their potential and be rewarded for their contribution to the success of the company.

True to the firm's corporate motto, the Markham community, customers, and employees are truly in "good hands with Allstate."

IBM CANADA LTD.

When IBM Canada Ltd. opened its headquarters building in Markham in 1982, it was a forerunner in Markham's business expansion, just as IBM has been a pioneer in the information processing industry.

For more than 70 years IBM has been doing business in Canada. Much has changed during that time. Its products have evolved from the time clocks and tabulating devices of the early years to the sophisticated information systems in use today. One factor, however, has remained constant: a dedication to helping Canadian organizations solve their problems through the effective use of advanced technology.

IBM Canada now has several sites in Markham. As well, Markham has become home to some 2,000 IBM employees and their families. Its existing headquarters building, together with an adjacent building scheduled for occupancy in 1991, will be the largest IBM non-manufacturing complex in the world. Also in Markham are the IBM Canada product distribution centre and a ser-

vice facility. In addition, IBM Canada has a country club in southwest Markham where employees, retirees, and their families enjoy recreational activities.

IBM's offices use technologically sophisticated support systems such as computer-controlled building environmental systems that monitor and

IBM Canada Ltd. employees, retirees, and their families enjoy a day of fun at the annual family picnic held at the firm's country club in Markham.

control energy use. The facilities also employ a system for reducing power demand charges and energy conservation features such as reuse of rejected heat from computers and high-efficiency glass.

Although part of an international organization, IBM Canada Ltd. enjoys a high level of autonomy. It is staffed and managed by Canadians. With more than 12,000 employees across the country, IBM Canada is a major employer, manufacturer, and exporter, with an annual gross income of more than $4 billion. As well, the company purchases about a half-billion dollars worth of goods and services from Canadian vendors and suppliers, many of them locally. As such, IBM

makes a substantial contribution to both Canada's and Markham's economic vitality.

The contributions that IBM and its people make touch many segments of the community. For instance, IBM believes strongly in enriching the quality of life in the communities where it operates and where many of its employees live. One way is through its Fund for Community Service. This program allows employees, retirees, and their spouses to obtain financial support for local non-profit organizations where they themselves volunteer their time.

IBM firmly believes in the value of education. It has invested millions of dollars in co-operative projects with Canadian universities. As well, the firm conducts thousands of days of customer and employee education annually. In the coming years much of that education will take place in a state-of-the-art education centre at its new Markham office facility at 3600 Steeles Avenue East.

IBM Canada Ltd. has played a pioneering role in the local business community. That role continues as the company helps Canadians use technology effectively to meet new challenges with confidence.

MARSHALL MACKLIN MONAGHAN LIMITED

Much of the pride a town takes in itself results from its urban landscape—the glass and steel, the transportation networks, and the parks. In Markham and other municipalities around the world, that pride can be linked to the engineering, surveying, and planning firm of Marshall Macklin Monaghan Limited.

For more than 25 years the firm has participated in the urbanization of Markham, helping to design and construct the buildings and infrastructure that converted a rural municipality to a major urban area.

That task is much removed from the company's first job in 1952, when University of Toronto professors O.J. Marshall and H.L. Macklin joined with P.A. Monaghan to conduct a pipeline survey in eastern Ontario. This led to the establishment, in an office in downtown Toronto, of a successful general surveying practice with a focus on the urban development industry.

In 1956 Marshall Macklin Monaghan moved its 200 employees to a new office building in Don Mills. Further growth necessitated another move in 1974, and yet another in 1990. The latest move, to a 70,000- square-foot, high-technology-oriented building in Markham, illustrates the firm's confidence in the

future of the town as a good place to do business.

Now employing more than 550 people, of whom one-third are registered professionals, the firm is owned and managed by its practitioners. This entrepreneurial structure allows it to identify, pursue, and take leadership in developing new market areas and projects in a way that is characteristic of few other engineering companies. The firm has broadened its consulting business to include pro-active management strategies that create financial opportunities for clients and itself. More than a quarter-century of experience has proven that its capabilities have reached beyond the boundaries of convention. The success of this approach became evident in 1987, when the firm was successful in obtaining Canada's largest airport construction project—the addition of a third passenger air terminal at Toronto's Lester B. Pearson International Airport.

Marshall Macklin Monaghan provides a multi-disciplinary consulting service to government and private-sector clients across Canada and overseas. Assignments have been carried out in the Caribbean, Africa, the Middle East, India, the Far East, Central America, South America, and the United States, as well as in all parts of Canada.

The nature of most assignments

undertaken by Marshall Macklin Monaghan necessitates the provision in one organization of a wide range of disciplines to comprehensively serve the needs of the client. The firm operates in the fields of municipal, environmental, waste management, water resources, structural, transportation, traffic, mechanical, electrical, industrial, and construction engineering; legal, geodetic, hydrographic and applied surveys, photogrammetry, geographic information services, remote sensing, and digital terrain modelling; and urban development, municipal, regional, economic, transportation, environmental and resource, tourism and recreation, and heritage resources planning, urban design, and landscape architecture. In addition, interdisciplinary skills include project management, environmental assessment, market and economic analyses, and computer sciences.

Throughout it all, Marshall Macklin Monaghan's approach has been to assemble the best in Canadian expertise. The firm's strength is its people, and the search for the best and most qualified is a continuing one. MMM professionals must be experts in their fields, as well as problem solvers and managers. They must be experienced in working as individual consultants, as part of a small group, or on a large multi-disciplinary consulting team.

Marshall Macklin Monaghan has been involved, in no small way, in the challenging task of facilitating the rapid urban growth experienced by Markham during the past few decades, and it is ready to participate in the town's growth for many years to come.

167

MILLER THOMSON

Sometimes it seems as if Toronto's Bay Street financial district has moved to Markham. Along with the commercial banking centres, lawyers, stockbrokers, and accountants have opened offices in Markham's glass and chrome towers. One major downtown law firm had the foresight to be the first to see the potential of Markham as a secondary corporate/financial hub for the Metro Toronto area.

Miller Thomson was founded in 1957 in Toronto. The firm's primary objective has always been to provide its clients with the highest-quality legal services in all facets of the law. Its Bay Street location has given it a corporate focus, but it stands behind a commitment to both personal service and reasonable cost.

In achieving these goals, the firm has enjoyed sustained growth in its client base and the depth of its expertise. Part of that growth involved the installation of an office at Woodbine and Steeles in Markham in 1981. Since that time the office has moved twice more due to continued growth. Today, in 9,000

Seated (left to right): Rod McLeod, Jud Whiteside, Peter Kiborn, David Moxon, and Ray Kallio. Standing (left to right): Michael Shell, Eduardo Barradas, and Wayne Gray.

square feet in the prestigious Scotiabank Commercial Tower, Miller Thomson is the largest professional services legal firm in Markham.

The firm is engaged in a wide area of practice that is especially useful to the increasingly sophisticated Markham business community. Practice areas include corporate and commercial law, securities, banking, real estate and administrative law, income tax, estate planning and administration, trusts, management labor law, litigation, environmental, competition law, bankruptcy, and hospital administration law.

Whether clients require assistance with incorporation or financing of their business, corporate acquisitions and mergers, or review of Competition Act compliance programs, Miller Thomson can help. Commercial clients range in size from corporations listed on national and international stock exchanges, to sole proprietorships, and include both domestic and international companies involved in all forms of business, sport, and community undertakings. The firm advises financial institutions, brokerage firms, and investment advisers in securities matters as well as represents banks and trust companies. Numerous clients are represented in lending and related commercial transactions,

The Markham office is located at highways 404 and 7.

Miller Thomson occupies 9,000 square feet in the Scotiabank Commercial Tower.

and administrative law expertise that has also added to its national reputation as a law firm representing several local, national, and international companies and organizations in a variety of environmental and other regulatory matters. The firm also has experience in private arbitrations and international business litigation.

Miller Thomson is as committed to the Markham community as it is to assisting clients with legal issues. The lawyers are encouraged to be actively involved in their community. And the firm itself plays a positive role through sponsorships, donations, and community involvement.

More than 30 years after its founding, Miller Thomson has expanded its commitment to quality to the businesses and residents of the town of Markham. The firm's lawyers and support staff look to the future in much the same way as Markham's corporate and individual citizens look to their own futures. It is intensely proud of its past, yet stands committed to the progress and growth the future is sure to hold.

and the firm is involved in all major areas of federal, provincial, municipal, and international taxation and treaty matters.

With Miller Thomson's strength and depth in income tax and commercial law, clients also use it extensively for estate planning. The firm's lawyers are capable of providing integrated advice to clients planning their wills and tax and property succession problems.

Responding to the fast pace of development in Markham during the past decade, many of Miller Thomson's clients are domestic and foreign investors as well as real estate brokers, developers, and lenders. The firm has expertise in condominium and commercial leasing and is a member of the International Council of Shopping Centres.

Another area in which Miller Thomson has a national reputation is representing management in all aspects of labor and employment law. The expertise that the firm offers employers includes employment contracts, employment standards, occupational health and safety, workers'

compensation, human rights, and negotiation, interpretation, and administration of collective agreements.

Miller Thomson has recently added an extensive environmental

Once an airport for small aircraft, Buttonville Airport today is a centre for commercial commuters.

NEL NETWORK ENGINEERING LIMITED

Unlike some professional firms who have left their mark on the ever-changing Markham landscape, the work of NEL Network Engineering Limited is largely unseen. That is because much of the result of its efforts is buried underground. Working for Bell Canada and Classic Communications Limited, this engineering and consulting firm has been involved in the design and administration of the town's telecommunications infrastructure—the underground network that provides cable television and telephone service to new subdivisions and upgrades service in old ones. The firm also undertook the design and drafting for the underground conduit project that was part of the beautification of the old village centres of Markham and Unionville in the late 1980s.

Established in Markham in 1982, NEL provides professional, technical, and consulting services to the telecommunications and cable-television industries. It has developed extensive expertise in all types of cable communications systems through infrastructure design, project planning, electronic design, project management, licence applica-

Pictured here at a rewards ceremony are (from left) Lorraine McGivan, computer operator; Dave Bernardo, CATV designer; Hugh MacKinnon, operations manager; Dexter Grandison, supervisor; Carmela Ragona, CATV designer; K. Kirk Odabashian, P.Eng., president; and John D. MacMicking, vice-president.

tions, and financial modelling.

Along the way, it has carved a unique niche for itself by combining telecommunications and cable television, which were traditionally rival industries, into one business. As a result, NEL has developed a totally integrated capability in a variety of engineering and consulting functions in a number of interrelated fields such as telecommunications, cable television, radio and broadcasting, satellite, mobile/cellular telephone, and hydro distribution. The firm provides a wide-ranging spectrum of services, including preparation of system specifications, system architecture, and detailed engineering plans for tender and construction, inspection, and commissioning.

This unique way of approaching the industry has created spectacular growth for the company. It is an ap-

proach that resulted largely from the backgrounds of the founding partners, K. Kirk Odabashian, P.Eng., and John D. MacMicking. Odabashian, who has a bachelor of engineering degree from Concordia University in Montreal, spent eight years with Bell Canada in a number of technical and managerial key posts before he joined a telecommunications engineering/consulting firm in 1980.

MacMicking, on the other hand, started his career with Classic Communications Limited, the cable television firm that serves Markham and the rest of southern York Region. He later moved to Scarborough Cable and then to the same consulting firm where Odabashian was employed. When that company closed its Toronto office, Odabashian and MacMicking formed NEL.

Their unique approach also resulted from a vision, shared by both partners from the beginning, that the cable television and telecommunications industries would eventually converge. And sure enough, the vision is proving to be true, facilitated by the emergence of fibre-optic technology.

But back in 1982 the partnership had what the partners call "a no-frills start"—an experience that remains embedded in the firm's management philosophy. In spite of extremely rapid growth (beginning

CATV down link satellite antennas at Classic Communications Ltd.

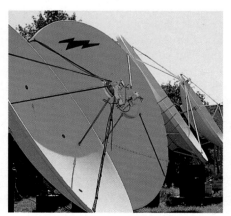

with 400 percent the first year and levelling off in the late 1980s at 40 percent), NEL has managed to retain the family-style atmosphere of its early days. Management by a supervisory group allows for a responsive and dynamic climate that attracts and retains skilled employees.

In the late 1980s the firm went through a restructuring process designed to help it deal with growth and position it for the future, which includes an aggressive expansion program through acquisition. The newly structured parent company, The NEL Group Inc. is comprised of NEL Network Engineering Limited, International Network Consultants Limited, and Internel Investments Inc. and employs more than 100 people. In addition to the head office in Markham, NEL has branches in Ottawa and Richmond

Hill, Ontario, as well as an office in London, England. The latter is part of the firm's positioning to operate internationally in a climate of expected European trade barriers beyond 1992.

In spite of this international focus, the modernization and extension of existing cable network facilities in the Markham and greater Toronto areas remains one of NEL's major projects.

Another project, of 11 years' duration, involves the Ministry of Transportation of Ontario. Working with the government's civil-engineering consultants, NEL is mandated to study and implement an innovative and futuristic freeway traffic management system. The interactive system, which employs state-of-the-art fibre technology, is the flagship of M.T.O.'s program.

NEL also plays a major role in the Ontario Ministry of Culture and Communications' Television Extension in Northern Ontario (TENO) project. As a consultant to the minis-

The executive team at NEL Network Engineering are (sitting) K. Kirk Odabashian, P.Eng., president, and (standing) J.D. MacMicking, vice-president.

try, its role included developing eligibility and criteria, providing assistance in the preparation of an applicants' handbook, evaluating more than 300 submissions, making recommendations for acceptance, and conducting post-construction audits.

In concert with a number of international and Canadian consultants, I.N.C. played a key role in the preparation of cable television licence application on behalf of Hutchison CableVision Limited. The $5-billion capital undertaking, unparalleled in the world, proposed a fully integrated telecommunication and cable television network, using state-of-the-art digital fibre technology.

Other companies on its client list include Northern Telecom, IBM, Rogers Cable Communications Inc., CUC Limited, Hutchison CableVision Limited (Hong Kong), City Centre Communications Inc. (UK), Ministry of Communications (State of Israel), and Canadian Satellite Communications Inc.

That list is destined to continue growing as The NEL Group Inc. carries out its commitment for the future: to provide a widely integrated group of services with a focus that continues to broaden beyond merely providing engineering/ design and into management. It is a plan that the Markham firm's partners hope will establish it as a substantial player in a global market.

A CAD training session (from left) Colleen Elste, technician; Lloyd Campbell, instructor; Steve Michalicka, technician; Janice Mumford, technician.

TKM

When TKM moved to its new corporate head office building in Markham, it required a three-storey crane to move a number of expensive computers into the second-floor computer centre due to a yet-to-be-completed elevator installation.

That tense scenario typifies the practical, find-a-solution-and-get-it-done-well spirit of this young, success-

The exterior and interior of TKM—a high-tech setting for a high-tech company.

ful, entrepreneurial organization. A relatively new member of Markham's high-technology industry, TKM is a privately owned Canadian corporation that was among the first companies in Canada to qualify for association with IBM as a business partner/authorized agent. In that capacity the company specializes in the IBM System/38 and AS/400 family of mid-range computer systems.

Managing the business within that relatively narrow niche, the company has developed a high level of expertise and a significant national reputation and offers a broad range of related products and services to a number of the area's corporations. Its reference list of clients includes the public sector, financial institutions, and many *Fortune* 1,000 companies within Canada and abroad.

Products and services are offered to prospective clients through a four-unit business structure: Systems Integration (analysis, conver-

sion assistance, custom systems, programming, and education); Enterprise Systems (the marketing, implementation, and ongoing support of Business Planning and Control System, [BPCS,] an integrated financial/distribution/manufacturing packaged software solution installed at more than 4,000 companies worldwide); Communications (telecommunications consulting and networking products and services); and Office/Legal (word-processing and integrated text management products, services, and related education for general industry as well as packaged software solutions for the legal industry). This approach allows both management and staff to continually expand their expertise and efforts in their areas of specific focus, with the customer as the beneficiary.

The company was founded in early 1984 by four individuals with a common interest and vision of a window of opportunity. Beginning opera-

tions out of a basement with two quickly secured high-profile accounts, the firm experienced business successes that saw it outgrow no less than six facilities over the next four years. TKM Inc. now employs in excess of 100 people and occupies a 20,000-square-foot facility on Highway 404 adjacent to the Buttonville Airport in the Valleywood Business Park. In addition, it has a 5,000-square-foot branch office in Burlington, Ontario, and the office/legal business unit is located on University Avenue in downtown Toronto.

TKM's strong business position today can be attributed to its tight market niche strategy and, within that, an unwavering focus on developing expert capabilities. Sound management has also played a major role. The philosophy has been one of recruiting and building on a team of well-rewarded, industry-experienced senior employees.

Growth continues to exceed annual projections, with sales increasing from one million dollars in the first year to more than $15 million in the fifth year. And the future?

TKM is committed to the IBM AS/400 and the considerable performance and benefits to come in that leading-edge technology. Management has aggressive growth plans and a "stick-to-the-knitting" mission: "To do more of what we know and do well and expanding our capability to be the only and last computer-services vendor a customer will ever need."

Photo by Mel Reid & Associates

CHAPTER ELEVEN

Building Greater Markham

From concept to completion, Markham's building industry and real estate professionals shape tomorrow's skyline.

Aries Construction Management Limited, 176-177; Cedarland Properties Limited, 178-179; Johnston & Daniel Limited Realtor, 180; Century 21 Armour Real Estate Inc., 181; Peter L. Mason Limited, Realtor, 182-183; Slough Estates Canada Limited, 184-185

Photo by Glen Jones

ARIES CONSTRUCTION MANAGEMENT LIMITED

For Greg Hoover and his ancestors, Markham has been a place of opportunity.

For his ancestors Markham offered escape from religious persecution in their native Switzerland. Settling in the community in 1804, they farmed the land and were able to practice their Mennonite faith and way of life under the tolerance of the British Crown. Since then, many generations of Hoovers have made Markham their home, with Greg being a seventh-generation member of the family's Markham lineage.

In 1981 Greg and his wife, Christina, founded Aries Construction Management Limited, a firm that provides construction management services to developers and corporate clients.

The Hoover family's long Markham heritage has had a profound effect on the corporate philosophy of Aries Construction. Greg Hoover's pride in his family's almost 200-year association with Markham has resulted in a strong sense of community obligation, which is embodied in the work of Aries Construction.

Growth is not the main objective of the company. Its principal

The Shoppes at the Promenade commercial offices and shopping centre on Bathurst and Centre streets, on old Highway 7, in Thornhill, Ontario.

goal is to provide work of the highest quality that will be viewed proudly for many years to come and to be known as an organization dedicated to excellence. The firm believes growth will come as a natural result as this goal is realized.

Prior to establishing Aries Construction, Greg had spent a dozen years as a project manager in the industrial/commercial construction business. During the latter half of this period, his responsibilities increasingly took him to many locales across the province. But in order to spend more time with his family and realize a longtime ambition, he decided to launch his own construc-

tion management firm. Greg believed that Markham was the ideal location in which to realize this professional ambition, not only because the community was experiencing the beginning of a commercial/industrial development boom, but also because of his ancestral roots.

For the first several months following its inception, Aries Construction operated from the basement of the Hoover family's Markham residence. A telephone answering machine served as a receptionist as part of a very low operating budget that was necessary to get the company up and running.

During the first three years of its existence, Aries Construction was engaged primarily as a general contractor for small-size commercial/industrial renovations. Its responsibility was to co-ordinate and supervise all facets of the renovation process. Aries successfuly completed numerous renovations for Brewers Retail, Loblaws, Cadillac Fairview, and various other recognized corporations provincewide.

As the company quickly earned a reputation for quality construction,

The 130,000-square-foot industrial/commercial development on Leslie Street at 16th Avenue on Richmond Hill in Ontario.

The interior and exterior of the Beth Avraham Yoseph Synagogue on Clark Avenue in Thornhill, Ontario.

Working in co-operation with a building owner, the firm helps develop a construction budget and schedule, examines alternative methods and materials, and suggests possible cost savings, all with the owner's input in order to achieve the best possible product for the least amount of expense.

Some of Aries Construction's significant construction management projects include Thornhill's Beth Avraham Yoseph Synagogue and the exclusive Shoppes at the Promenade retail complex, the Yonge Street/

the size and scope of its renovation projects assumed a greater dimension. Some of its prominent renovation projects include the head office of National Grocers in Brampton, Ontario; the head office of construction for Loblaws Supermarkets in Toronto; and the head office of the Cadillac Fairview Shopping Centre development in Toronto's Eaton Centre.

The beginning of a new corporate direction for Aries Construction occurred in 1984, when the firm coordinated and supervised the construction of its first free-standing structure—a 40,000-square-foot industrial building in Scarborough. Since then, the majority of the firm's business has been in the construction of free-standing new buildings.

As a co-ordinator and supervisor of construction projects, Aries Construction has taken a significant departure from the traditional approach of general contracting. The firm offers its services on a consulting basis, separate from the construction budget of a project. In this manner, a building owner can rest assured that Aries will co-ordinate a bal-

ance between quality workmanship and the construction budget both in the best interest of the owner.

By acting as a construction consultant, Aries Construction is able to develop a strong two-way relationship with its clients. As a result, it can better understand and meet their needs, as well as offer them greater budget flexibility and control.

Unlike the traditional scenario in which a general contractor becomes involved in a project only after architectural and engineering plans are completed and construction is ready to begin, Aries Construction's service is available from a very early conceptual design phase.

York Mills Avenue Loblaws supermarket in Toronto, and the North York head office of The Glen Group development firm.

From its beginning as a husband-and-wife operation, Aries Construction Management Limited has grown into a thriving firm that relies heavily on the experience and integrity of its office and field staff, operating out of its facilities in Markham's Valleywood Corporate Centre. More important, the firm has given Greg Hoover the opportunity to make a contribution to a community that has played an integral role in the growth and well-being of both his immediate family and his ancestors.

CEDARLAND PROPERTIES LIMITED

It must have seemed like a whim to the development industry in southern Ontario when, in the early 1970s, an upstart firm acquired a 700-acre farm in the country north of Steeles Avenue and south of the village of Markham. But that visionary purchase from the farm equipment manufacturer Massey Ferguson Industries was to set the stage for the metamorphosis of Markham from a sleepy, rural village to a booming metropolis.

The firm that made that pioneering purchase was Cedarland Properties Limited. It was incorporated in 1972 as a result of a partnership between Rudolph Bratty, Q.C., a lawyer, and Stanley Leibel, a land developer. In the next two decades Cedarland Properties and its various corporate divisions helped shape Markham through an extensive program of industrial, commercial, and residential developments. The program turned Cedarland into one of the area's major developers and builders.

Cedarland serviced and developed that first 700 acres of land, then sold a portion as commercial and industrial property with the balance residential housing, thus beginning what is now the massive Milliken Mills area of Markham. That same process of development and resale continued until 1979, when the firm broadened its scope of activity and built its first neighborhood shopping plaza on Warden Avenue, just north of Steeles. With the successful completion of the plaza, Cedarland began a pattern of diversification, involving itself in the industrial, commercial, and residential construction businesses.

The privately held firm has Rudy Bratty's stamp firmly imprinted on it. As managing partner, he has put in place an effective management structure that has allowed the company to grow and prosper while financing many of its major industrial developments internally through its own resources without having to arrange mortgage financing. The philosophy dictates short

lines of communication with direct responsibility being given to the managers involved in each of the firm's divisions: industrial and commercial construction, residential construction, land development, finance and administration, property management, and mortgage administration.

Communication is kept as simple as possible in order to avoid errors in decision making arising from miscommunication. Support staff in each area is technically qualified and has been molded into an efficient and fast-acting team that can respond quickly to opportunities or changing circumstances as they arise. The team acts as a management focal point for more than 100 corporate and noncorporate entities.

Cedarland leases a substantial portfolio of industrial buildings. Some of the major tenants include IBM Canada Ltd., Tie Communications, Toshiba Canada Inc., Kubota Tractors Ltd., Tupperware Canada Inc., Office Equipment of Canada Inc., Semi-Tech Microelectronics, and American Express Canada Inc.

In 1989 the firm completed construction of the 340-suite luxury Markham Suites Hotel that stands as a landmark at the southwest corner of Warden and Highway 7. In addition, two retail projects have recently been developed. The Kennedy/Denison Supercentre Plaza has 190,000 square feet of mixed retail space anchored by a massive Loblaws Supercentre grocery store. And a huge market-type, specialized retail project called Market Village-Markham is being constructed by Cedarland in joint venture with another partner.

Under its residential housing division, the company builds a large volume of homes each year. And in the 1990s the firm is further diversifying into condominium construction with two towers being built at Highway 48 and Steeles Avenue that will initially be rented or sold. Although its area of concentration is Markham, it has residential projects under way in virtually every major

centre from Scarborough and Ajax in the east, to Mississauga and Brampton in the west, and north to Barrie. Its residential housing division is one of the most efficient residential builders and has the highest

sales volumes.

The future looks just as promising for Cedarland Properties Ltd. A large inventory of prime serviced industrial commercial land is held in Markham, ready for future construc-tion and expansion of its income-producing property portfolio. And a further large holding of acres of un-serviced and partially serviced land is waiting for future residential expan-sion.

The Markham Suites Hotel, a 340-suite lux-ury hotel, is a Cedarland Properties devel-opment that stands as a landmark on the corner of Warden and Highway 7.

JOHNSTON & DANIEL LIMITED REALTOR

who married a man named Sabiston, inherited the old homestead and kept it in the family until the mid-1980s, when a new commercial development changed the face of the landscape again. The house, however, escaped the fate of the neighboring homes, which were demolished. Johnston & Daniel had it renovated, maintaining its original character and charm, while at the same time creating a beautiful, efficient, and professional office setting.

The house's enduring solidity typifies the Johnston & Daniel Limited

The Johnston & Daniel Limited Realtor office is located in an historic house on Highway 7 in Unionville.

An historic house on Highway 7 in Unionville symbolizes the enduring quality of the service provided and properties sold by the real estate firm that uses it as an office.

Since 1950 Johnston & Daniel Limited Realtor has built a reputation as a highly specialized residential real estate company that markets premier quality residential properties in the Metro Toronto area and the Muskoka district. An active office is also maintained in Unionville to serve Markham and surrounding areas.

In 1969 James R. Gairdner joined the company as one of its 22 sales agents and a year later became its president, setting the tone for the future growth and style of the firm. Employees look upon Gairdner as a caring, concerned, hands-on president who is always available for help. His management style is participative, with every manager being a vice-president and involved in decision making. Agents are regularly thanked and rewarded at gala affairs, Christmas parties, and family picnics in Muskoka.

Under Gairdner's direction, Johnston & Daniel has expanded to 250 sales representatives and brokers in 11 branches, including the Markham/Unionville office. The firm is completely computerized for financial

purposes and is compatible with the Real Estate Board's on-line computer system. A strong program of corporate advertising helps market the company as well as individual properties.

The Town of Markham is well served by an office in the historic Sabiston House. It was part of the original tract of land owned by the town's founder, William Berczy, in the 1700s. The property was secured by the Eckardt family around 1800, at which time the existing board and batten home was replaced with a more sturdy brick structure of mid-Victorian design. Eckardt's daughter,

Realtor's commitment to the highest standards of fairness and ethical practices for its clients, salespeople, management, and staff. The firm's excellent reputation is also a reflection of its involvement as a corporate citizen with support being regularly given to charitable and community organizations, large and small. They range from the major health charities and hospitals to the Toronto Symphony and National Ballet. Life in Markham is enhanced by the support of events such as public school raffles and sponsorship of local sports teams and events.

CENTURY 21 ARMOUR REAL ESTATE INC.

Despite the fact that Markham has experienced a highly competitive real estate market during the past several years, it would be difficult to find many neighborhoods without at least one home displaying the familiar Century 21 Armour Real Estate "For Sale" sign on its front lawn. In fact, Century 21 Armour has been among the Century 21 organization's top five Canadian sales producers since 1982.

The success story behind the firm began in 1972, when lifetime Markham resident Doug Meharg opened Armour Real Estate to better serve the needs of the public as an independent broker. Meharg possessed a thorough knowledge of the local marketplace. He had sold commercial and industrial real estate in the area for several years. Prior to that, he operated as an independent builder and developer in the community for more than a decade.

Meharg's familiarity with the local market, coupled with a strong en-

Douglas Meharg, president.

thusiasm for the real estate business and the desire to provide clients with a high level of service, enabled Armour Real Estate to grow steadily during its first few years of operation. But he realized that the firm, as an independent brokerage, would eventually face expansion limitations. Time and manpower constraints would limit the number of new agents that could be recruited and properly trained each year.

Consequently, in 1977 Meharg decided it was time for the company to enter a partnership with the Century 21 International organization. This meant that the business would continue to be independently owned and operated, and thus maintain its strong community roots. But it would gain many benefits from being part of a franchise network with more than 7,000 sales offices and 125,000 agents presently throughout the world.

The Century 21 organization would provide Armour Real Estate with ingredients such as staff training and support, national advertising programs, client referral systems, and proven methods in managing corporate growth. There was also the increased public recognition that came from being part of the organization.

The business relationship has proven to be a resounding success. In addition to impressive sales figures and a reputation for knowledgeable and conscientious service, Century 21 Armour has been able to drastically expand the size of its sales staff. When it first became part of the Century 21 network, the firm had a dozen sales agents. It now employs a sales force of about 90 at its Markham office alone. A second location, in Unionville, has an additional 40 agents.

Not only has Century 21 Armour Real Estate Inc. enabled Doug Meharg to achieve his original aim of better servicing the needs of the local real estate market, it has also given individuals from all walks of life the opportunity to realize their career goals and personal potential in the process.

Standing in front of the new head office—opened in May 1988—at Highway 7 East and Cosburn Road are vice-president Sue Meadows and president Douglas Meharg.

PETER L. MASON LIMITED, REALTOR

The explosion of development in Markham over the past decade has not been a casual occurrence. Rather it reflects a sensitivity on the part of the municipal government, developers, and their agents to the needs of an increasingly sophisticated business and residential community.

With both residential and non-residential space in great demand, landlords and tenants, developers, and purchasers alike all need a resourceful and reliable real estate firm. That is the role carved out for itself by Peter L. Mason Limited, Realtor, a firm that has opened the doors to some of the finest residential, industrial, and commercial properties in southern Ontario.

Peter Mason has real estate in his blood, having grown up surrounded by the excitement of the industry. He started in the business with his father's firm, Webb and Mason. When his father accepted a position at York University in 1967, it seemed natural for Peter to start his own operation. That was the beginning of an impressive career, fuelled by a vision that the tremendous level of interest in Markham farmland would eventually lead to unprecedented development.

That original two-person company has now grown to employ close to 90 people, and much of its success can be attributed directly to those individuals. The essence of Peter L. Mason Limited is a staff of

Above: Dorothy Mason, vice-president/residential division, and Peter L. Mason, president.

Below: Pictured on the lawn of Peter L. Mason Limited's head office are some of the company's sales and administrative staff—90 strong and growing.

Scotiabank Commercial Tower (165,000 square feet) is part of a major office/ hotel development in the heart of Markham. The next phase will be the three-tower atrium-linked 350,000-square-foot Bull Corporate Centre, leased by Peter L. Mason Limited.

skilled, trained, and highly motivated professionals, well equipped to serve clients with a full range of computerized real estate services. They are also extremely loyal to the firm, many having shown long-term commitment by becoming shareholders. There is a low rate of employee turnover, which is unusual in the real estate business.

The ICI division, which is most active in the Markham area, is located near the Don Valley Parkway and Highway 401 Interchange in order to efficiently serve clients in Markham, York Region, and Metro Toronto. Another strategic organizational move came in 1987: Peter L. Mason Limited became the Canadian affiliate of New America Network, Inc., the largest affiliation of independent commercial and industrial real estate brokers in the world. The network provides a unique capability to market properties internationally, through the strength, depth, and expertise of its affiliates in major and secondary markets throughout Canada, the United States, Europe, and Asia.

In spite of the firm's international contracts, it has its roots in Markham. President Peter Mason, SIOR, FRI, PLE, has lived in Markham since he was a teenager. He grew with the community, and he and his wife, Dorothy, a Markham native, have raised four daughters

there. Both the Masons and their company maintain a strong sense of civic pride, from assisting local youth recreational programs through sponsorship of curling, hockey, and baseball teams, to active involvement with the Markham/Stouffville Hospital. Peter Mason himself is a director of the hospital's foundation board, and was first chairman of the board of management of the Markham Theatre for Performing Arts and chairman of its fund-raising committee. He and Dorothy have both been active in The Markham Board of Trade, with Dorothy being a past president.

Although the company is active throughout Metro Toronto and surrounding regions, it has maintained a special interest in Markham as seen by its dominant presence in the town. Its major Markham project has been the marketing of a 40-acre development at the intersection of highways 404 and 7. The project, which will have more than 1.2 million square feet of space when completed, comprises seven structures, including the Scotiabank Com-

mercial Tower, the Bull Corporate Centre, and the Valhalla Inn Markham.

The company has also sold the land and is marketing one of the finest office parks in Canada, the Markham Town Centre Business Park, which stretches from the new Civic Centre to Rodick Road, north of Highway 7.

To further assist corporate clients, Peter L. Mason's residential division was formed in 1977 by Peter's wife, Dorothy. Specializing in both community and estate residential properties, the company's personnel are highly skilled in relocations, corporate transfers, and individual moves. Located in the heart of Unionville, it has built its fine reputation by adhering to the same professional principles and high standards that have always guided the firm.

Like Peter Mason's commitment to the community of Markham, his dedication to his career in real estate has heavily involved him with the volunteer side of his industry. He has worked tirelessly to improve its professional ethical standards, a task that saw him rise to the position of president of both the Toronto Real Estate Board (the largest in the world) and the Ontario Real Estate Association. He and other executives of the firm are also active in numerous other business organizations. In addition, Mason has received three prestigious real estate designations: member of the Society of Industrial and Office Realtors, fellow of the Real Estate Institute of Canada, and member of the Association of Land Economists.

The firm's hard work and dedication to professionalism have been integral to the development of Markham. Peter L. Mason Limited, Realtor, has seen, in 25 years, the price of serviced industrial land rise from $14,000 per acre to more than one million dollars per acre. But the same degree of care has been given to all deals, whether small, individual sales or multimillion-dollar corporate transactions.

SLOUGH ESTATES CANADA LIMITED

It began in 1970 with an ambitious series of low-rise industrial buildings carved from a cow pasture. But within a decade that field was to become the entrance to one of the country's most prestigious business locations.

Slough Estates Canada Limited was a pioneer in Markham, one of the first companies to initiate development when Canada's Silicon Valley was not even a dream in a developer's subconscious. The visionary international developer had the foresight to purchase prime land on what it knew would be the extension of the Don Valley Parkway and begin construction there of its Markham Industrial Park.

The 415,000-square-foot industrial portion of this 19-building, 37-acre development was, a few years later, complemented by three office buildings consisting of 300,000 square feet of prime space on eight acres. True to the pioneering vision, the entire project is now ideally positioned to provide access to Toronto and the rest of the province's markets.

Fully integrated 24-hour security is provided for office tenants. There is ample parking, plus truck access to shipping areas, along with professional landscaping that enhances the visual and working environment.

Although Slough has many properties in Markham, they are only a small portion of its extensive holdings, which are international in scope. Slough Estates Canada Limited is a subsidiary of Slough Estates PLC, a United Kingdom real estate group with international operations.

Slough Estates Canada Limited develops, owns, and manages industrial and office parks in Toronto, Markham, Mississauga, Brampton, Montreal, and Vancouver. In Markham, Slough Estates has close to 30 buildings with more than 100 tenants.

The British company is one of the largest international property development and investment companies in that country.

Founded in 1920, the firm pioneered the design/build concept for Europe. After World War II ended, it decided to diversify to other countries in order to offset the risk inherent in being dependent on the economy of any one country. Recognizing the potential of expanding its scope of development to countries such as Canada, Australia, and Belgium was also a decision of foresight: Slough Estates has since maintained an unbroken record of profit growth. Current international holdings in the United Kingdom, Canada, the United States, Australia, Belgium, France, and West Germany total close to 40 million square feet.

The Canadian company, which was established in 1950, develops, owns, and manages industrial and office parks located in Toronto, Mark-

ham, Mississauga, Oakville, Brampton, Montreal, and Vancouver. Historically, Slough's rental properties have been well-located industrial buildings with some office content. More recently, however, Slough has increased its portfolio of pure office buildings. The locations chosen tend to become major centres of business activity, wherever they are located.

The philosophy behind Slough's property business is that by leasing or renting premises, tenants avoid the necessity of committing valuable capital resources to bricks and mortar, thus releasing funds for more productive investment in their own businesses. So when Slough decides to locate in an area, it does so with the knowledge that, as both developer and future landlord, it will become a long-term participant in that community.

As a major owner of suburban property, Slough Estates is very conscious of its responsibilities to the community, the environment, and the local economy. It therefore has a commitment to maintain high standards of building design and property management. All the buildings are developed and managed in a controlled park environment with a high standard of property maintenance and landscaping. In so doing, the firm is able to attract a large proportion of excellent tenants, many of which include major corporations who see the wisdom of leasing rather than owning their premises. And so it is in Markham, where Slough Estates has close to 30 buildings with more than 100 tenants.

Just north of the original Markham development is a 22-acre site known as Slough Park Bentley. It contains single-storey, campus-style offices and traditional industrial-type structures. In this 290,000-square-foot complex is a combination of industrial and office space designed to meet the ever-growing and expanding needs of the Markham business community. A high level of comfort, security, and cost efficiency is available to all tenants—from the largest corporate giants to the smallest professional firms and business offices.

All these projects have led to the recognition of Slough Estates as one of the major developers of the second half of the twentieth-century—and one that has remained just ahead of the leading edge of progress in Markham. The Slough vision is still in gear, and the Markham Industrial Park is currently undergoing a redevelopment and facelift to keep pace with changing times. In recognition of the shifting emphasis in Markham from industrial space to prestigious office buildings, two industrial structures are being demolished and in their place is rising a 12-storey, 240,000-square-foot office tower.

The combination of Slough's expertise and experience, backed by significant financial strength, enables it to continue to create and capitalize upon new business opportunities as they occur.

CHAPTER TWELVE

The Marketplace

Markham's retail establishments, service industries, and products are enjoyed by residents and visitors to the area.

Photo by Dawn Goss

PROVINCIAL GRAPHICS INC.

A Heidelberg six-color half-web.

When Provincial Graphics Inc. opened its doors for business in 1973, it had two main assets that would enable it to become one of Canada's largest privately owned printing companies with full-color production capability.

The first asset—a used, single-color printing press—was an obvious prerequisite. The second asset, however, was not as tangible, and was something that the company's employees were more apt to notice and appreciate than anyone else. It had to do with the corporate philosophy of the firm's president and co-founder, John Warbutton.

Immigrating to Canada from his native England in 1955, Warbutton tried his hand at various jobs until he entered the print business and subsequently became the manager of a printing plant. Provincial Graphics was born eventually from his desire to become self-employed.

The company became one in which there is an unusually high degree of mutual respect between all levels of co-workers, and one in which individuals do their best to share knowledge instead of hoard it. In order to promote equality, very few Provincial Graphics employees indicate corporate titles on their business cards, including Warbutton himself. Another result of the firm's "people come first" philosophy is that no one has ever been laid off.

Even though Provincial Graphics has grown into a firm with a staff of 100, a family environment pervades. By striving to maintain a healthy balance of experienced employees and younger ones who are attuned to new trends and ideas, the company has been able to perpetuate a sense of vitality and enthusiasm.

In addition to its "people" philosophy, Provincial Graphics has made a large investment in superior technology, enabling it to manufacture quality products and to become part of the print industry's upper echelon. Nothing can better attest to the firm's rise to the top than its spectacular growth in revenue. In its first year of operation, sales were $277,000; when Warbutton acquired full control and ownership of the company in 1983, that figure had increased to $4 million.

Since then, the company's annual revenue has soared to above the $20-million mark.

In order to meet the growing needs of its clientele, Provincial Graphics has made several moves to larger premises over the years. When the firm first began doing business—following a start-up investment of $4,000—it operated from a 2,500-square-foot facility in Scarborough, Ontario. In 1978 it moved to the first of its three Markham locations, which contained 10,000 square feet of floor space. Five years later came the move to a facility that was more than twice as large as the previous one, followed by the 1987 relocation to its present address on Cochrane Drive, which provides 45,000 square feet. In 1986 Provincial Graphics opened Magnalith Inc., a film-processing division also located in Markham and employing one-quarter of the total corporate staff.

As Provincial Graphics moved to larger facilities, a key feature of its printing plant operation remained the same. Since day one, the firm has been committed to using strictly Heidelberg printing presses, which are among the most expensive on

The board of directors at Provincial Graphics Inc.

the market. Presently, all seven of its various presses are German-made Heidelbergs, printing everything from full-color annual reports, corporate brochures, and pictorial books to art reproductions, posters, and advertising material. Known for their reliability and ability to print high-quality material, Heidelberg presses are so highly regarded by the print industry that their value generally appreciates as they get older.

By standardizing its brand of presses, Provincial Graphics is able to bring greater efficiency into its production plant, which turns out printed material 24 hours a day. Standardization makes it simpler for press operators to learn how to operate all of the company's presses, ensuring that the costly machines are handled with expertise and care, and that they can be serviced regularly with little difficulty. Press malfunctions and breakdowns—which can be a catastrophe for printing companies—are consequently minimized and quickly remedied. Because Provincial Graphics prints a

The headquarters of Provincial Graphics in Unionville.

large number of annual reports, it is crucial that their timely distribution to corporate clients is not in any way hindered by mechanical problems.

With many of Provincial Graphics' clients being large companies, advertising agencies, and design studios, print production of the highest quality is the norm. As a result, capital expenditures on equipment capable of producing such material is astronomical. While Provincial Graph-

ics spent $26,000 on its first press, which was secondhand and had only single-color capability, its proudest acquisition was a brand-new Heidelberg half-web press costing approximately $4 million.

Fed from a large roll of paper, the half-web can print 40,000 sheets per hour, containing four full-color pages on both front and back. Its color reproduction capability is so great that it is comparable and at times superior to the reproduction quality of sheet-fed presses. Termed as a six-color press, it reproduces colors such as gold and silver, as well as special blends of solid colors that might be used as distinct corporate colors or in corporate logos.

With about two-thirds of Canadian demand for printed products being in the Metro Toronto area, Provincial Graphics Inc. has accomplished remarkable growth in a fiercely competitive market—and in a relatively short period of time. Undoubtedly, its president's vision of a harmonious and humanitarian work environment, coupled with a strong emphasis on quality and service, have been essential ingredients to this print industry success story.

Provincial Graphics has made a large investment in superior technology, enabling it to produce superior quality products.

189

MARKHAM SUITES HOTEL

Considering Markham's rapid transformation into a bustling commercial centre and the fact that it is home to numerous corporate concerns from all corners of the globe, the concept behind the Markham Suites Hotel is a first-class idea.

Opened in early 1989, the hotel and its 332 suites have been designed with particular attention to

The Unionville Cafe provides Markham Suites' guests elegant, comfortable dining.

the needs and expectations of business professionals. At the same time, however, the hotel also caters to a diversity of guests, ranging from vacationing families to foreign travellers.

Each suite in the Markham Suites Hotel offers a bright, comfortable living area and separate bedroom, as well as two desks—each equipped with a telephone—two color television sets, and a mini-bar. The environment is ideal for those who need to host small meetings, work on a business project, or entertain guests in a comfortable setting.

Secretarial service is available, and there are also photocopying, Telex, fax, and in-room computer hook-up facilities.

One of the most distinctive features of the Markham Suites is its unique architectural style, which utilizes a 10-storey glass atrium as the hotel's focal point. From the exte-

rior, a magnificent glass clock tower rises the full length of the building's front facade, while on the inside, there is an art-deco atmosphere amid light-colored marble, exotic flora, and splashing fountains.

A number of the hotel's larger suites have windows that open onto the atrium, while others—which boast more than 1,200 square feet of floor space—offer amenities that include a spacious living room and dining room and a wet bar for personalized catering.

The Markham Suites has 13 meeting/banquet rooms, the largest able to accommodate 400 people. An elegant 72-seat restaurant features fine French cuisine and is complemented by the Unionville Cafe and a piano bar lounge. Situated off the second floor of the hotel is a Japanese garden—complete with flowing fountains, bridges, and picturesque trees—which is ideal for receptions or barbecues.

Guests who stay at the Markham Suites receive free access to the Markham Suites Health Club. The state-of-

Light-colored, reflective marble and soft lighting highlight the Markham Suites Hotel lobby hallway.

The Markham Suites Hotel's unique architecture utilizes a 10-storey glass atrium, art-deco-style furnishings and interior design, marble floors, and splashing fountains as its focal point. Shown here is the hotel lobby.

the-art facility offers an indoor pool and whirlpool, five international squash courts, computerized weight-lifting and exercise equipment, aerobics classes, saunas, a private spa, and club masseuses and masseurs.

As with any first-class hotel, the Markham Suites realizes that it is often the extras that contribute to a pleasurable stay. Located on the premises are a florist, gift boutique, elegant clothing shop, and a hair salon. There is also parking space for 700 vehicles.

Conveniently located in the geographic heart of Markham and minutes away from most of the area's businesses, the Markham Suites Hotel provides the first-class lodging facility local residents and visitors have come to expect.

LE PARC BANQUET AND CONFERENCE CENTRE

Le Parc-Markham.

One indication of a community's sophistication is the amount and quality of conference and meeting space it has developed. Until recently Markham had very few such facilities of any quality. Now that it has developed into a high-quality corporate and residential centre, it also has an abundance of first-class meeting and banquet space.

One facility in particular sets new standards. Le Parc Banquet and Conference Centre opened in 1988 near the centre of Markham's corporate activity at highways 404 and 7. From the distinctive, low-slung granite, glass, and brass exterior to the spacious foyers with light filtering through the foliage in greenhouse-style windows, Le Parc is an elegant yet efficient showcase that lends an air of class to any function.

It can accommodate more than 2,000 people at one time in six halls with more than 45,000 square feet of banquet, convention, and meeting space. Whether the event is a

meeting for 50 people, a theatre-style presentation for 1,500, or a wedding banquet for 1,100 in the 15,000-square-foot main hall, Le Parc can carry it off in style.

Le Parc's management office regularly buzzes with activity as bookings come in, often more than a year in advance, for both business functions and family gatherings. A conference co-ordinator is available to facilitate the planning of conferences and meetings. All the backup facilities are in place to ensure events run smoothly, from a loading dock for trade shows to state-of-the-art kitchens. Le Parc's management has endeavored to create a hotel atmosphere, complemented by a reputation for high-quality food served in generous portions.

Part of that reputation derives from the accolades showered on La Reserve, an elegant Continental restaurant that is part of the complex. This 140-seat dining room maintains its own high-quality wine selection, prides itself on exemplary service, and also contains two intimate private dining rooms.

The Le Parc concept was developed in 1981 when a group of developers and business people opened the first banquet hall with the same name, a few miles to the west in Concord. As large traditional weddings came back into fashion and the business community grew, sales tripled in the first four years, and the banquet hall was expanded. And as Markham developed in the late 1980s, the second Le Parc came into being.

The Markham site is further enhanced by the emergence of two six-storey granite-and-glass office towers. With 100,000 square feet of quality commercial and office space, these buildings further demonstrate Le Parc's foresight and complete its support of both the Markham corporate and residential communities.

191

SUNKIST FOOD MARKETS

In 1972 Sunkist Food Markets owners Jack Comella and Angelo Pugliese caught a glimpse of the future—and since then, they haven't looked back.

Foreseeing that Markham would become a fast-growing and prosperous community, the two partners acquired a parcel of land that year near the intersection of Woodbine and Steeles avenues and opened their second fruit market. Their new store proved to be so successful that by 1979 it was rebuilt and enlarged. But, more important, their move to Markham signalled the beginning of a new chapter in Sunkist Food Markets' corporate evolution.

The first Sunkist Food store was opened in 1929 by Comella's uncle, Sam Comella, and his partner Sam Badali. Located on Danforth Avenue in Toronto's east end, it became renowned for consistently offering fresh, top-quality produce and a high level of customer service. When Badali retired in 1950, Sam Comella took over the business and, a decade later, upon his own retirement, passed the reigns to his son.

In 1967 Jack Comella, who had been working for Sunkist Food Markets for several years, purchased the business from Comella's son and brought his friend Angelo Pugliese into the fold. As new owners, they stressed the same approach to quality and service as Sunkist's founders had done for many years prior—and added a few touches of their own.

Sunkist Food Markets soon became one of the first fruit markets in Toronto to remain open 24 hours a day—ironically, because it had become too time consuming to move ever-increasing quantities of merchandise in and out of the store each day. And, in order to make their produce look more appealing and to protect it from the sun, the two partners began placing large, brightly colored umbrellas above it. Both innovations were well received

by Sunkist's clientele, and business kept growing.

In 1984 a new store was opened in Mississauga and, in 1988, a second one in Markham at Markham Road and 16th Avenue. Following the partners' decision to become a specialty supermarket operation, the Danforth Avenue store was sold in 1986. While quality produce and attentive service remain the foundation of the Sunkist Food Markets chain, each location now offers a wide range of grocery products as well as a bakery, delicatessen, meat counter, and fresh pasta and salad bars.

Topping off the growth Sunkist

Quality produce and attentive service remain the foundation of the Sunkist Food Markets chain, with each location offering a wide range of grocery products as well as a bakery, delicatessen, meat counter, and fresh pasta and salad bars.

Food Markets has enjoyed since coming to Markham, it was chosen for the Best Business Gold Award in its category in a major market survey in 1988 and 1989.

Just as the original Sunkist store became a well-known and appreciated fixture of Toronto's east end, Markham's Sunkist Food Markets outlets are well on their way to becoming the same.

DON VALLEY NORTH TOYOTA

On the surface, Markham's Don Valley North Toyota doesn't seem much different from many other dealerships across Canada. Like some counterparts, it sells automobiles and trucks that are manufactured by the Toyota Motor Corporation of Japan. As well, it displays shiny new vehicles in its showrooms and has a knowledgeable and courteous sales staff, highly trained service technicians operating from state-of-the-art mechanical facilities, and a well-stocked parts department.

The difference is that Don Valley North Toyota is the showcase dealership and window on the Canadian marketplace for Yokohama Toyopet Co. Ltd., one of the largest independent dealerships for Toyota products in the world.

Opened in 1973, when Toyota vehicles were just becoming a major force in Canada, Don Valley North Toyota was the result of the foresight of chairman Kanji Miyahara, who correctly foresaw the global nature of the automobile industry.

The dealership was to provide Yokohama Toyopet a vantage point from which it could readily observe

the needs and preferences of the Canadian marketplace. This would enable the company to learn how to better serve consumers and employees who were becoming increasingly global in their values and lifestyles.

The knowledge and experience thus obtained, when combined with the parent company's wealth of same, has resulted in large-volume sales and excellent standards of customer service. In both the home market and in Canada, this venture

Don Valley North Toyota.

has provided the company, its employees, and its customers with benefits even beyond the expectations of its founders.

When it selected the location of its flagship dealership, the firm's choice of Markham of the early 1970s proved an ideal site. It has been the company's philosophy to reinvest any gains in the development of the local business and the betterment of the local community.

Don Valley North Toyota has consistently been the top-selling Toyota dealership in the country—in terms of both the number of new cars sold annually and dollar volume.

In 1982 Don Valley North Toyota opened a sister dealership in Markham, known as Markville Toyota. The two dealerships operate as individual entities and employ about 150 people. In 1988 the company opened its collision repair center on John Street in Thornhill.

From a corporate point of view, and undoubtedly for many satisfied Toyota owners, Markham's Don Valley North Toyota has played a valuable role in the sales of Toyota vehicles to the Canadian marketplace.

Markville Toyota.

HUNT PERSONNEL

In today's competitive business environment, companies are increasingly realizing that the quality of people they hire has a significant impact on how successful they will be. As a result, they have placed more emphasis than ever before on staff recruitment and hiring procedures.

But finding and selecting the most qualified candidates for various employment positions takes considerable time, effort, and expertise. Many companies have found it advantageous to turn to employee placement agencies for assistance in this critical function.

In the Markham area, Hunt Personnel has been a leader in the employee recruitment and placement field for more than a decade. In addition to serving the full-time placement needs of a wide array of local clientele, the firm, through its Temporarily Yours division, specializes in temporary help placement.

Founded by Toronto native Ted Turner in 1967, Hunt Personnel operates a combination of 15 franchised and company-owned offices from coast to coast. Its Markham office opened in 1978 and since 1982 has been owned and operated by area resident Dianne Ramster.

Temporary help placement constitutes a major portion of the business Hunt Personnel conducts with its Markham clientele. At any given time the firm has more than 150 temporary field staff working for businesses throughout the local area. As many of Markham's corporate concerns are service oriented in nature, the type of temporary help they require most from Hunt Personnel is secretarial and clerical staff, word-processing and typing specialists, receptionists, computer operators, and bookkeepers.

One of the fastest growing industries in North America, the temporary help field offers many benefits to both employers and employees.

By adopting temporary help as an integral part of their corporate strategy, businesses can maintain their productivity in a cost-effective manner during crucial periods. For instance, the need for temporary help might be prompted by factors such as changing technology, seasonal workload fluctuations, special projects, rush jobs, emergencies created by unforeseen terminations, absenteeism, changing production schedules, and maternity leaves.

For employees, temporary work

can offer a career with a variety of different corporate environments or the flexibility to accommodate a lifestyle not based on full-time employment. It can also provide the opportunity to learn new professional skills, make extra money, or be employed while searching for an ideal full-time position. And because employers' needs for temporary help might be sudden or necessitate specialized skills due to changing office automation technology, temporary employees often command wages higher than their full-time

Left: A team approach to client/candidate matching is key to Hunt success.

Below: At Hunt Personnel computerized testing and skill upgrading eliminate guesswork.

counterparts. If an employee and employer wish to move to a full-time work arrangement from a part-time one, Hunt Personnel will do everything possible to make the transition a smooth one.

In order to assist businesses in selecting the most suitable temporary employee to operate specific office automation software, Hunt Personnel deploys a unique testing program known as FOCUS. The program can objectively analyse and upgrade individuals' skill levels on more than a dozen different business software packages. Testing can also be customized to match employers' specific data-entry formats.

In the area of full-time placement, Hunt Personnel is dedicated to offering long-term support and value to its clientele. For example, the firm's consultants are paid a salary as opposed to commissions and strive for long-term results instead of quick placement. This system also enables consultants to utilize a team approach in placing job candidates, giving candidates access to all suitable positions available through the firm, regardless of which consultant they deal with.

Hunt Personnel's role in the employee placement process includes paying for and co-ordinating advertising, screening telephone and written responses from candidates, conducting interviews and skill tests,

checking references, and matching candidates' abilities and experience to a job's particular requirements. Once this tedious process is completed, the firm usually sends no more than two candidates to a prospective employer.

Therefore, human resources managers evaluate only the most qualified prospects, saving time and expenses involved in the interviewing process. Moreover, time saved can be devoted to important functions such as planning employee resources, producing staff development and training programs, and conducting personnel evaluations.

Compared to an employer who directly interviews a candidate for a job, Hunt Personnel, as a third party, can obtain information from job candidates that is much more objective in terms of frankness and opinion. This leads to a quicker and more accurate assessment of a candidate's suitability for a specific job. In addition, if the firm finds an indi-

vidual who would fit well in a certain corporate environment or position, it will, on its own, recommend that individual to a client.

Hunt Personnel guarantees both its temporary help and full-time placement services. Clients who use the firm's temporary workers always receive a follow-up call the first day the employee begins working for them, with subsequent follow-up calls on a weekly basis. In the case of full-time placements, Hunt Personnel will replace a newly hired employee, free of charge, up to six months from the time they start working for a client.

Through offering conscientious service and long-term value, Hunt Personnel has played a key role in the personnel requirements of many Markham businesses. And until the day arrives when people stop being the most crucial element in any business, Hunt Personnel and its reputation will continue to grow and prosper.

This salaried team specializes in the Markham/Unionville area.

MARKHAM VILLAGE LANES

As a focal point of downtown Markham's Main Street, Markham Village Lanes offers a fine example of traditional charm blended into a modern-day shopping environment. Nestled between several refurbished nineteenth-century dwellings, many of Markham Village Lanes' retail shops and offices overlook a charming open-air courtyard. Throughout, there pervades an array of peaked roofs, paned windows, and old-fashioned street lamps. A steepled tower rises proudly above the complex, recapturing a bygone era with its heart-warming chimes.

The first phase of Markham Village Lanes, which includes the historic Wilson and Browning homes, opened in 1985. Two years later the facility was purchased by Rethberg Ltd., a company owned by West German-based interests. A third historic dwelling will be added to the rear of the complex in 1990, housing additional retail shops and offices.

In addition to its classic charm

and convenient location, Markham Village Lanes offers a shopping environment with a high level of personalized service. Its retail shops, all independently owned and managed, offer everything from clothing, shoes, and giftware to flowers, gourmet food, and wine.

During summer months the courtyard of Markham Village Lanes is transformed into a picturesque patio where shoppers and visitors can sit down to have a refreshment and often be entertained by local musicians and variety performers.

As much as Markham Village Lanes is an integral part of downtown Markham's commercial and professional development, its historic dwellings played vital roles in the community more than a century ago.

A fine example of Victorian architecture, the Wilson House was built in the 1880s by Henry Wilson, a well-known local merchant. In 1917 it was purchased by Dr. John MacDonald to be used as his residence and place of practice. It subsequently housed the practice of his daughter, Dr. Innis MacDonald, one of the first women in Canada to

The steeple at Markham Village Lanes, a focal point of downtown Markham's Main Street.

earn a medical degree, later to become a noted eye specialist. The house remained in the MacDonald family until 1983, when it was sold and renovated extensively.

The Browning House was built in the 1840s as the home of William Browning, who conducted his clock and watch repair business from the dwelling. It also housed Markham's first telegraph office, operated by Browning's daughter. The home was used as a recruiting office during World War I and was purchased in 1920 by the Markham Women's Institute to serve as a library, which remained in operation until 1967.

Markham Village Lanes, like its predecessors, will develop a unique tradition as time goes by. In the meantime, it will be a focal point of downtown Markham and offer an intimate shopping experience.

The historic Wilson House in the courtyard of Markham Village Lanes.

MARKVILLE SHOPPING CENTRE

One of the events that marked the evolution of Markham from a small town to a sophisticated municipality was the October 1980 ground breaking for Markville Shopping Centre.

The shopping centre opened in 1982 with 150 stores, restaurants, and services, including Eatons and Woolco department stores. Eight years later an expansion anchored by Simpsons and The Bay raised the number of stores to more than 250. Markville has provided hundreds of jobs for local residents. As well, it has consolidated under one roof all stores and services essential to a family's shopping needs. Today Markville has become a comprehensive, regional one-stop shopping centre.

The elegant two-level centre provides the shopper with a very pleasant atmosphere. Natural light pours in through skylights while the greenery creates a year-round summerlike atmosphere. The refreshing sound of flowing water emanates from an indoor stream that empties

into a fountain, which is located in the spacious centre court. When shoppers are hungry, Markville's food court offers a variety of foods for taking out or eating in. Restaurants and department store cafeterias round out the dining choices.

The many clothing stores at Markville ensure that shoppers no longer need to travel to Toronto for designer fashion. The shopping centre prides itself on offering a wide selection of fashionable clothing for the entire family. These fashions are showcased four times per year in fashion shows geared to appeal to varied tastes.

The woman who has been with Markville since its inception is general manager Eugenia Cork. She is dedicated to enhancing the shopping experience. Eugenia Cork has made Markville a centre for commu-

Markville is the flagship property of JDS Investments Ltd., a company founded by president Jack Israeli more than 30 years ago to create residential and industrial development.

The centre court at Markville Shopping Centre. Photo by Bruce Hogg

nity activity. Space is provided for promotional displays and activities for many local organizations, ranging from food banks to youth groups and charities. Many other activities take place in the centre, including craft shows, travel displays, antique and home shows, school art displays and performances, a volunteer day, and seasonal celebrations.

Markville is the flagship property in the portfolio of JDS Investments Ltd., a company launched more than 30 years ago by its president Jack Israeli. After the successful development of what is now Eaton Sheridan Place in Mississauga, Israeli developed other shopping centres in Pickering, Cambridge, North York, and Sudbury. In 1988 JDS acquired Canada's Wonderland, a major entertainment and theme park just west of Markham. The planned future development of the Wonderland site, and the continuing growth of Markville Shopping Centre, are all part of the efforts of JDS to assist in the development of Toronto's surrounding regions in conjunction with the demands of its residents.

AMERICAN EXPRESS CANADA, INC.

Just as the American Express Card is one of the world's best known instruments of purchase, American Express Canada, Inc., is one of Markham's most prominent corporate citizens. Its massive head office on McNabb Street employs a staff of more than 2,200, and oversees a wide range of service products in Canada, including charge cards, travellers' cheques, insurance services, and more than 120 travel service offices.

American Express Canada is a wholly owned subsidiary of the U.S.-based American Express Company, which was formed in the early 1850s to transport goods and mail across the North American continent. Following the establishment of express lines into Canada, the company opened offices in Toronto and Hamilton in 1853.

As North America's commercial and financial needs expanded, the firm introduced new facets to its freight-forwarding and travel businesses. The year 1882 brought the invention of the American Express Money Order, a financial instrument that offered security and conve-

nience to replace the risks of cash. In 1891, after a company executive encountered difficulty with a letter of credit while on a business trip, development was initiated of an instrument that would be as safe as the traditional letter of credit but easier to use. The result was the American Express Travellers' Cheque.

By 1898 the first of the organization's more than 1,600 travel service offices was opened. Spanning the globe, the network has enabled American Express to become the world's largest travel agency. It wasn't until 1958 that the first American Express Card was issued. Today the card is used by more than 30.7 million card members and is honored by 2.5 million retail establishments in more than 130 countries.

One of the founding principles of the American Express organization states that active corporate citizenship is beneficial for the company, as well as its employees and the communities in which it operates. As a result, American Express Canada supports many artistic, cultural, educational, and charitable endeavors, on both a local and national level. By supporting artistic and cultural events, American Express contributes to the economic health of the communities in

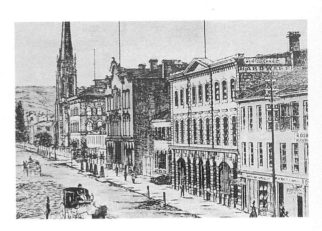

The first American Express offices in Canada were located in Hamilton, Ontario.

which it does business and helps to promote Canada as a travel destination.

Among the local organizations that American Express Canada supports are the Markham Theatre, The Markham Board of Trade, Markham-Stouffville Hospital, Markham Kiwanis, the Senior Games, Junior Achievement, and various youth athletic teams.

World renowned for its developments in the financial services field, as well as being a corporate citizen that supports a wide variety of groups and causes, American Express Canada, Inc., is truly a Markham business leader in every way.

The Canadian headquarters for American Express Canada, Inc., which is located in Markham.

GREENBELT MOTORS

Gerd Reisenecker, owner of Unionville's Volkswagen/Audi dealership, says, "Our product line has a strong market penetration in this area. This reflects the fact that the people living here are a bit out of the ordinary—they identify with quality product and service."

Reisenecker is himself a bit out of the ordinary, and Greenbelt Motors bears his unmistakable stamp. Using a winning blend of innovation and humor, one of his first moves after taking over the dealership in 1981 was to sponsor a car at the Mos-

Greenbelt Motors, a service-oriented Volkswagen/Audi dealership, is located on a two-acre site adjacent to a planned interchange for the new Highway 407.

port race track—a good publicity move made even better by the fact that the car sponsored was a Formula Ford.

But Reisenecker's philosophy is most evident in the fact that the dealership is famous for its service orientation. That emphasis is not surprising, given his background as a mechanic in his native Germany and automotive technician teacher at an area community college. He has, in fact, built upon the strong Volkswagen reputation for service by using his technical background to improve quality control and mechanic selection.

This upgraded service creates a feeling of confidence in the minds of customers who know their vehicles will be repaired economically and properly. In addition, Greenbelt employees—from service advisers and mechanics to receptionists—can be counted on to add that extra little touch, whether by supplying rental cars, driving customers to work locally, keeping the service department as clean as the showroom, or participating in the community by sponsoring youth sports teams and festivals.

The philosophy works: Revenues

and staff have more than quadrupled since 1981. But Reisenecker isn't the type to let things stagnate. He has built Greenbelt's parts department into the second-strongest wholesaler in the Metro Toronto area. And just a few years after establishing the Volkswagen dealership, he spent more than $600,000 on renovations to add the Audi dealership. Then he expanded the used-car sales part of the business and added a division that leases all makes and models of automobiles, on both an individual and fleet basis.

Then Reisenecker decided his service was not complete unless he could repair the bodies of cars as well as their mechanical workings. Thus evolved the Greenbelt Collision Centre, which operates in a separate facility a few miles across town. The body shop offers everything from total reconditioning and frame straightening, to minor body repairs, downdraft painting, and professional corrosion protection.

Reisenecker's second decade as a Volkswagen/Audi dealer should be as successful as his first. Greenbelt Motors is ideally poised to continue to grow along with Markham—its two-acre site is right beside a planned interchange for the new Highway 407.

VALHALLA INN MARKHAM

"Warmth is more important then bigness," an unusual slogan but one that represents the philosophy at each Valhalla Inn across Ontario.

But warmth is more than a word; it is an attitude expressed by all the people that work at Valhalla. "What could be more important to a traveller than warmth and friendliness expressed by service personnel in the hotel, fine food and service, quality accommodations—all the ingredients of a Valhalla Inn," suggests Peter Peachey, president of Valhalla, who, with Carl Binder, executive vice-president/hotels, heads up the corporate office management team responsible for operations.

Warmth and hospitality are Valhalla's trademarks. Patrons can find other hotels with similar facilities, but they won't feel as comfortable. Valhalla Inn is not just a hotel; it is a total experience.

The original Valhalla Inn was built in the City of Etobicoke in 1963 and since that time has become a landmark. The name "Valhalla" comes from Norse mythology describing the place that the god Odin and his warriors returned to

at night. Using the original slogan, "Hospitality under the Triple Roof," the Scandinavian-designed hotel was built of natural materials such as brick, wood, stone, and glass surrounding a beautifully landscaped courtyard that became a trademark of the Valhalla Inn.

The silhouette of the triple roof became the company's corporate logo. Valhalla expanded into Kitchener, Thunder Bay, and, most recently, Markham.

The $25-million Valhalla Inn Markham is strategically situated at the intersection of highways 404 and 7. The design of the 15-storey, 208-room hotel fits in with the surrounding high-technology area, but still exhibits the distinctive timbered, triple-roofed dining area and lounge. The majority of Valhalla's business comes from corporate training and seminars. The hotel has a two-level conference centre with a separate entrance and foyer. There are eight meeting and banquet

Peter E. Peachey, president of the Valhalla Companies Limited.

rooms and five executive boardrooms. Soon Valhalla Inn Markham will have a lush central garden courtyard, extensive recreation facilities, and first-class food and beverage operations.

However, the Valhalla experience is much more than facilities. The philosophy of warmth is embodied in a management style dedicated to making the guest experience a satisfying one. This is accomplished largely through staff members whose attention to detail, appearance, and attitude reflect an extra feeling of pride and commitment. This Valhalla devotion to quality has been recognized, for seven consecutive years by the CAA/AAA through its prestigious Four Diamond Award for outstanding service and facilities.

For Valhalla Inn Markham, the future holds continued steady and well-planned growth. The warmth of a family-owned business with special attention to details, and design and selection of materials keeps people coming back year after year.

The Valhalla Inn Markham.

Photo by Dawn Goss

Patrons

The following individuals, companies, and organizations have made a valuable commitment to the quality of this publication. Windsor Publications and The Markham Board of Trade gratefully acknowledge their participation in *Markham: Canada's Community of the Future.*

Allstate Insurance Companies of Canada
Alpine Electronics of Canada, Inc.
American Express Canada, Inc.
Aries Construction Management Limited
Assinck Bros. Limited
Blake, Cassels & Graydon
Burndy Canada Electronics Division
Cedarland Properties Limited
Century 21 Armour Real Estate Inc.
Chesebrough-Pond's

(Canada) Inc.
Cyanamid Canada Inc.
Deloitte & Touche
Don Valley North Toyota
Ford Electronics Manufacturing Corporation
Glynnwood Retirement Residence
Greenbelt Motors
Hanna Paper Fibres Ltd.
Hunt Personnel
Hyundai Auto Canada Inc.
IBM Canada Ltd.
Johnston & Daniel Limited Realtor
Le Parc Banquet and Conference Centre
Levi Strauss & Co. (Canada) Inc.
Markham Hydro Electric Commission
Markham Suites Hotel
Markham Village Lanes
Markville Shopping Centre
Marshall Macklin Monaghan Limited

Peter L. Mason Limited, Realtor
Miller Thomson
Mitsubishi Electric Sales Canada Inc.
NEL Network Engineering Limited
OE Inc.
Pannell Kerr MacGillivray
Peat Marwick Thorne
Petroff Partnership Architects
Provincial Graphics Inc.
Raywal Limited
Shouldice Hospital
Slough Estates Canada Limited
Sunkist Food Markets
TKM
Toronto Airways Ltd.
Town of Markham
Valhalla Inn Markham

Participants in Part II, "Markham's Enterprises." The stories of these companies and organizations appear in Chapters 8 through 12, beginning on page 121.

Bibliography

Chapter One

Champion, Isabel. *Markham 1793 to 1900*. Markham: Markham Historical Society, 1979.

German Pioneers of Toronto and Markham Township: The Story of William Moll Berczy. Toronto: Historical Society of Mecklenburg Upper Canada, 1976.

Markham Economist and Sun. Untitled news story, November 30, 1939.

Markham Economist and Sun. Editorial, February 9, 1950.

Marshman, Paul. "Who'd Want to Stop the Steady Stream?" *Markham Profile*, Fourth Edition (1986): 29-32.

"Planners Anticipate Boom Development." *Markham Economist and Sun*, August 18, 1977.

"Rapid Change in Markham Township Foreseen by Reeve." *Markham Economist and Sun*, January 12, 1967.

Women's Institutes of Ontario, Unionville Branch. Multiple unspecified authors—ongoing collection. Unionville: Women's Institutes of Ontario, 1969.

Chapter Two

Leddy, Sheilagh M. "Markham Planning has Power." *Markham Economist and Sun*, November 14, 1973.

"Markham." *Yorktech Directory*. Markham: Alcoma Communications, 1985.

"Markham The Hub of the Golden Circle." *Markham Economist and Sun*, June 23, 1960.

"Minimum Assessment." *Markham Economist and Sun*, November 1967.

Peter Barnard Associates. *Population and Employment*. Markham: Town of Markham, August 1983.

"Village Council Reduces Tax Rate Two Mills." *Markham Economist and Sun*, August 8, 1940.

Chapter Three

"Another Major Industry." *Markham Economist and Sun*, April 13, 1967.

Champion, Deb Bodine. "Planners Give Go Ahead to Proposal." *Markham Economist and Sun*, June 25, 1988.

"Development Breaks Records." *Showcase Markham '88*. Unionville, Ontario: Toronto Business Magazine, June 1988.

Markham Profile. Markham, Ontario: Markham Board of Trade, 1986.

Town of Markham. *Annual Report*. Markham, Ontario: 1988.

Chapter Four

Champion, Isabel. *Markham 1793 to 1900*. Markham: Markham Historical Society, 1979.

"Markham to Lend Builder up to $500,000 for Hall Renovation." *Markham Month*, February 1985: 12-13.

Piper, Angela. "Big Plans for Markham Main Street." *Markham Month*, October 1985: 25.

"Special Report: The Town of Markham." *Business & Finance in Ontario*, Vol. 2, No 12, October 1984.

Suite Talk. Markham, Ontario: The Markham Suites Hotel, 1988.

"Town Council Approves Markville." *Markham Economist and Sun*, August 25, 1977.

Town of Markham. *Annual Report*. Markham, Ontario: 1988.

"Wedding Cake House—a Pioneer." *Markham Economist and Sun*, September 8, 1977.

Chapter Five

"Construction on Target." *Markham Economist and Sun*, June 16, 1977.

Cowan, Phyllis M. "Markham's Strength." *Markham Board of Trade Profile*, Spring 1986: 50.

Markham Museum: Learning to Discover the Past. Markham, Ontario: Markham District Historical Museum.

Murphy, Tony. "Unionville Main Street." *Markham Board of Trade Profile*, Spring 1985: 76.

Stecyk, Vic. "Historical Thornhill." *Markham Board of Trade Profile*, Spring 1985: 81.

Stevens, Victoria. "Buttonville at a Crossroads." *Toronto Star*, June 28, 1988.

"Tremont House Furor Spawns New Society." *Markham Month*, June 1986: 13.

"U.C.D.S. Group Fights for the Community." *Markham Economist and Sun*, November 7, 1973.

Chapter Six

Champion, Isabel. *Markham 1793 to 1900*. Markham: Markham Historical Society, 1979.

"Public Meeting Endorses Pool Complex Project." *Markham Economist and Sun*, March 4, 1976.

Resident's Guide. Markham, Ontario: The Town of Markham, 1987.

Winter Guide. Markham, Ontario: Markham Parks & Recreation, January 1989.

Chapter Seven

Champion, Isabel. *Markham 1793 to 1900*. Markham: Markham Historical Society, 1979.

FitzGerald, Doris M. *Old Time Thornhill*. Thornhill, Ontario: 1970

"Markham Grows Up." *Markham Economist and Sun*, November 7, 1973.

Piper, Angela. "Commitment to build." *Markham Profile*, Spring 1985: 40.

"Report on M.H.S." *Economist and Sun*, May 31, 1945.

"Union Villa—A Centennial Project of Unionville Home Society." *Markham Economist and Sun*, November 9, 1967.

"Union Villa bungalows will be first of a kind in Canada." *Markham Economist and Sun*, August 9, 1979.

Index